URBAN MYSTIC

Ancient Wisdom
from a Modern-Day Seeker

CHRISTOPHER DESANTI

Jo,
I am beyond grateful!
Thank you for everything! Love ya
Enjoy

[signature]

Light of Awakening Books
DELRAY BEACH, FLORIDA

Published by:
Light of Awakening Books
DELRAY BEACH, FLORIDA

Copyright © 2018 Christopher DeSanti

ISBN-13: 978-1-7321484-0-6

Production by The Book Couple • TheBookCouple.com

Printed in the United States of America

CONTENTS

∞

INTRODUCTION

The path my life took makes perfect sense to me now, but when it was all starting to take shape, I couldn't have planned for it to look the way it does today. Working with people on a weekly basis to help transform their lives, traveling internationally, and holding classes and trainings over the years for thousands of people wasn't what I thought my life would be about, and yet this is what it is.

It began as a deep yearning, a calling that I responded to as though I were in a dark room following flickers of light that led me to interesting places, places rich with wonder and wisdom. Each part of my experience has been integral to the whole, and that is what this book, *Urban Mystic*, is about. It's about giving you, the reader, insight into what I've observed and learned so that it can ultimately be applied to and understood in your own life.

This book is a culmination of what I have experienced on my journey so far—in my own words and from my own observations. It doesn't come from any one modality. As you read this book, you may find spaces opening up for you to see what's being pointed to in your own heart, your own mind, and your own day-to-day experience. I have attempted to not repeat myself, but certain concepts and distinctions are repeated in this book as necessary to share my observations. Ultimately, it is all pointing to the same thing throughout—because the Truth is One.

This book isn't about pushing a new dogma or another set of beliefs on you that you will need to learn and practice. My intention is to be able to pass my insights on to you through these words so that you can open yourself to receiving insights of your own—to think critically, and through that, to clarify for yourself what is being presented. In many ways, you are a participant in the writing of this work; you are authoring these words as you interpret their meaning for yourself. When you see these ideas clearly, once they are distinct, meaning that they stand on their own, they can then be a powerful catalyst in your life. May you enjoy this book, and may it light a fire for you on your journey.

And by the way . . . none of what I say is the Truth.

THE AUTHOR
OF OUR OWN STORY

We live in quite an interesting time, and although we could say that we have more than our ancestors had ever dreamed of, we are faced with challenges that are affecting the very fabric of our lives, world, and future. In the midst of all of the technology designed for connecting, knowing, and experiencing our world, many people are facing a dark time in search of what is sacred for themselves. In this time of *more,* many are feeling like *less.*

As a seeker after truth and someone who has continually challenged the cultural and societal program of my own mind, I can relate. I also have some key observations that, when contemplated and applied, can offer you powerful openings of possibility and awakening.

I have spent more than twenty years of my life on this path of awakening—which has included both challenges and victories—and, during the process, I have come to regard myself as an urban mystic. Why an urban mystic? Because of my love and quest for knowledge, and because I am a product of what might be called an "urban" culture—a culture that has ventured far away from the simplicity of hand-to-mouth living, a culture that glorifies the fast-paced city lifestyle of lights, money, power, and sex.

I grew up not far from New York City, which I came to learn contains nothing that has not been developed by human beings. Every single thing in that city has been created by our technology—from the subways to Central Park, all of it was designed by us. I am very clear that we are in need of something sacred, something that is within each of us and yet seems to have been forgotten. This something can awaken us from the sense of loneliness and fear that many of us are feeling in these precarious times. These feelings stem from the confusion of warring and conflicting ideals between what is important and valuable to us and what is not.

A parroting of spiritual concepts and paradigms, which has become the norm in today's definition of spirituality, is not what we need right now. Many people know and can recite what all of the books and teachers have been saying for thousand of years, but when it comes down to the simple application of those teachings, many still seem lost.

I trust that my words can be a tool for you because I am like you. I don't come to you as a teacher, but rather as a friend and brother who has experienced all of the beauty and ugliness of what it means to be human, just like you. I am not interested in being a guru or someone who is "special" in the eyes of others. We have seen enough of that, and I can tell you that I have learned a lot from fallen masters, self-proclaimed enlightened teachers who profess to have the answer but whose lives behind closed doors seem to be anything but enlightened.

These times call for something new, where we gently turn away from the path of power and elevation over others and the world and allow a gentle, quiet compassion to arise within us. Though the essays to follow are written from my perspective, they are about what brings you alive personally. If you would be with my simple yet powerful observations, you can use them as keys to awaken something within you. Take your time with them, reflecting and contemplating as you read each one.

We must recognize ourselves as the author of our own story and the hero of our own journey. So, in many ways, this book is about you, the journey you are on, and how you and I are similar. I give you these words so that they may be a signpost for you, a pointer from a man who walks on the same path of life that you do, someone who is simply sharing his observations and experiences so that you may more readily see yourself as the perfect manifestation of what it is you have always been looking for.

MY STORY

The story began in wonder.

As a child, I realized a few things about myself early on. First, I could pick up new things quickly and excel at most of them. My mother, who always makes me laugh, tells me that from the time I understood what words on a paper meant, I was always asking her to teach me to read. Something drew me to reading. Something about learning inspired me. When I was a kid, I was really only interested in learning about things that intrigued me, and, as it turns out, I was intrigued by *a lot* of things. Religion and God fascinated me early on, and I loved watching videos about Jesus and Biblical stories. Before I started to question everything I was being taught at Sunday school, I felt very moved and inspired by it. You could say that I was a seeker from the beginning.

The second thing I realized about myself is that, from a young age, I had a strong imagination, along with a photographic memory. In many ways, I actually felt like I had memories from other places, some of which I had never visited in this lifetime. I felt as if this wasn't the first time I've been here and almost as if this life was a continuation of something.

I lived my first few early years in wonder and joy, but I soon found myself trying to keep up with my older brother and his friends. I got bullied a lot (which was my introduction to the harsh realities of life), and I learned quickly that the way to earn the older boys' respect was to be good at sports. We moved to the next town over when I was about eight, and I felt relieved that I was no longer the little kid on the block.

Together, my brothers and I had a really great time growing up. Ours was a perfect little town with the perfect family and friends. We had great holiday traditions and played outside and in the woods most days. We biked and ran everywhere, and our lives revolved around sports. We had great friends with whom we are still close to this day, decades later. Life *really* was perfect.

∞

The sport that I was drawn to the most was basketball. Even though I also loved football and baseball, and excelled at them, I made a conscious decision to pursue only basketball because it felt like a calling and I was a natural at it. By the time I was in middle school, I was good, and by the time I graduated middle school, I was considered to be one of the best in the state for my age group. Basketball became an obsession, and I practiced with fury. It felt like I was able to capture a feeling within myself and express it when I was on the court. I went there to deal with challenges of life and also to be inspired. It didn't matter what was happening; the court became my sanctuary.

Michael Jordan was a huge influence on me. He was everything I wanted to be as a basketball player, and my section of the room I shared with my brother housed an enormous collage of Jordan pictures that everyone called "the shrine." My father would drive me to the courts late at night, park the car, and take a nap while I would put on my headphones and play in the dark by myself, listening to Yanni, a popular instrumental musician of the day, and visualizing myself playing like Jordan. The piano would take me away into another dimension. I didn't realize it then, but my spiritual journey was being forged on the basketball court.

∞

By the time I was fourteen and entering high school, I was invited to play on the varsity summer league. Even though my older brother and I were quite competitive with each other and he didn't want me to play varsity, he was on board to let me play with him after some strong persuasion from my father. My father, in many ways, lived vicariously through us as athletes. He was a proud father, and it showed; very rarely, if ever, did he miss a game. He was dedicated to us, so it was natural for him to convince my brother to let me play on the varsity team.

It was during the summer going into my freshman year that I felt as if I were closing an amazing chapter of my childhood journey and growing into what was next. That magical summer was one of the greatest I can remember. We merged with the other nearby towns for high school, and each day was filled with excitement for what would come next for us. New friends and old friends came together as we spent our days and nights in one another's company.

One day during that summer, a gentleman who had caught wind of how good I was at basketball came to watch me play. Following an awesome game, I played my next one while this man heckled me from the sidelines, shouting, "You can't play, kid! You can't shoot!" After a while, he took a seat next to me and asked, "You're getting frustrated out there, aren't you?"

I remember my exact reply: "Mister, leave me the hell alone!"

That was the last I saw of him that summer. It wasn't until later in the season of my freshman year, by which time I was not only starting as a shooting guard on the varsity but also became the leading scorer on the team, that one of the fans gave me an envelope that had been passed to him in the seats.

The envelope contained a business card and a newspaper article about a man who coached all of the top basketball talent in the state, talent that went on to great basketball schools and some into the NBA. I called the number on the card, and eventually my father and I went to meet the coach who was proposing that I play for him. It was none other than the same man who had been heckling me from the sidelines! I ended up playing for him as a result, and I got a chance to play against many top players at the time. I felt like my big break had come. I traveled weekly to different places around the country, playing against all of the best players. Shortly thereafter,

I was ranked as one of the top one hundred players in the United States for my grade. Considering I was only fifteen, it was really quite unbelievable.

But as beautifully as it had all come together for me, it just as beautifully fell apart. The coach urged me to change schools and head to a private school known for basketball, where I ended up having to sit out half the season because of a rule in New Jersey designed to prevent kids from transferring schools for sports. Nevertheless, the coach introduced me to many of the top coaches for division-one schools, but he pushed me harder and harder each day, driving me to a point where I lost my passion for the game. Everything became about where I was ranked and what schools were scouting me. The game I had once loved became a huge burden for me, more of a business than a game. I heard more yelling than cheering.

∞

The one moment that really changed the course of my life was when I learned that my parents were getting a divorce. Until then, everything had seemed perfect between them, but I quickly learned that it wasn't. My mother was unhappy, and although she attempted to work on the marriage with my father, eventually she made the choice to leave him. Even though I didn't fully understand, I trusted that it was the right move because I loved my mother.

My father used to pick me up from basketball practice at my new school and drive me home, often in silence.

His whole life had been turned upside down. Meanwhile, I was miserable, taking a train every day to an all-boys school where I missed all of my friends, just to sit out half of the season. To top it all off, my mother had just been diagnosed with breast cancer. So, in the matter of that one year, I went from living my dream of playing basketball in the perfect town with a perfect family to having it all come crashing down.

I was a wreck; I could barely play well, and I was miserable and lonely. I started talking to a therapist to help me with my pre-game anxiety. Then I tore one of my quadriceps and could not play the game I loved for the first time since I could remember. I ended up in physical therapy.

Until that time, I had been reading books and studying the deeper aspects of being an athlete. I found comfort in seeing what I was doing in basketball from a higher perspective. One day I asked a teacher in class if she had heard of a certain author whose book was at my house (I hadn't read the book, but it had caught my attention). My teacher had heard of the author and asked me to bring the book to school. The next day, as I sat on the train heading for school, I opened the book up and started reading it. The message of that book hit me like a lightning bolt. It was about a kid I could relate to and his spiritual journey. I felt as if the old saying, "When the student is ready, the teacher appears" had come to life for me.

The book itself wasn't as important as what was awakening inside me. I knew something had come to life deep within. It was an ancient calling, a light of awakening. I felt so excited and alive with possibility, with something new, and at the same time something very old, within me, coming to the surface. The journey home had begun, or rather was recognized. Looking back, I can see it was always there, but this was a pivotal moment.

Within a week, I decided to stop playing basketball for the all-star coach that recruited me and went back to my old high school. Although I had to sit out half the season again, I didn't care; I no longer wanted to play basketball professionally or even in college. I felt a calling awaken inside me that nothing was going to stop, and to this day, twenty-three years later, nothing has.

∞

With a new vision for myself, I began to read profusely. We didn't have Internet at the house back then, so I would often go the bookstore and research topics to delve into. My research led me to Native American studies, and I found myself walking in nature, often alone and barefoot. I felt the need to reconnect to the Earth. My brothers and I participated in sweat lodge ceremonies, sometimes in the dead of winter. The interesting thing about my journey was that although mine was quite specific to me, both of my brothers were also having similar experiences. It's as if we were all called at a young age. Somewhere deep in my heart, I believe this is an agreement we made prior to this life together.

My spiritual path shifted direction from the world of shamanism with the chance finding of *Be Here Now* by Ram Dass. I "happened" to be standing in my best friend's older brother's room and was drawn to that book on his bookshelf. *Be Here Now* opened me up to an entirely new world. I was mesmerized by Ram Dass's words, and through him and his teachings, I found incredible teachers whose knowledge has impacted me ever since, teachers like J. Krishnamurti, Ramana Maharshi, and Nisargadatta Maharaj, among many others. Their wisdom colored my days with wonder and joy again, this time on a different level. (Eventually, I was lucky to be able to attend an amazing one-day course led by Ram Dass during my senior year of high school. It was a great springboard for my journey.)

I read books in my high school classes that had nothing to do with what was being taught, much to my teachers' frustration. (In fact, a piece of chalk was thrown at me on more than one occasion.) I intuitively knew that I wouldn't use most of what they were teaching in my future, and something kept telling me that what I was reading and studying on my own would someday be of use to me.

I spent my college years living a fun, social life without basketball, at the same time reading and learning about the nature of life and consciousness. I majored in Human Development and Family Studies because I felt that was the closest field to what I was so interested in: really asking the questions and being in discovery of "Who am I?" I read everything I could get my hands on, the majority of it from the East, particularly from India. Tales of saints and sages, gurus and followers fascinated me.

In my early twenties, I journeyed to India for the first time to attend Satsang, a group meeting to ponder the nature of Self, with a well-known teacher at the time. This would be the first trip where I felt the opportunity to finally experience what I had been reading about for many years. The impact of that experience followed me through my twenties, and even though I found myself in many worldly pursuits, it was as though there was a place inside me calling me home.

∞

Right out of college, I landed a part in a major motion picture where I got to play myself being a tour guide in Cancun during spring break, which is what I happened to be doing anyway in Mexico for two months each year (between my trips to India). With this movie, I would be in the spotlight once again, but the spotlight was short lived; the movie opened in the Top-Ten worldwide and bombed. In many ways, I was living a double life during this time, on one hand seeking God and Truth, and on the other making my way in the world. Those two lives wouldn't merge until later.

Directly after the film, I found myself working in the mortgage industry and making money pretty quickly. I did that for nearly ten years, and it was a crazy time for me. Though I was still deep in spiritual learning and contemplation, I mainly kept it to myself. The mortgage industry, which I was thoroughly immersed in, eventually led me to move from New Jersey to Florida.

In 2008, in the blink of an eye, the whole industry

came to a crashing halt. I literally found myself wondering where my next dollar and meal would come from. At the time, I was in a relationship with someone I had grown up with. (She had played a big role in making the summer before high school so memorable.) Fast forward fifteen years, and we were living together in Florida and talking about marriage. Then, just like it had happened before, it all came falling down. This time, I went through a serious undoing, losing everything, including the townhouse my girlfriend and I owned together, as well as my condo on the water. My girlfriend and I split up as the times got harder. I started wondering what the purpose of my life was going to be.

As part of my healing following these losses, I decided to attend a healing center that focused on the teachings from India with which I was so familiar, combined with *A Course in Miracles*. I knew of the *Course* and had read parts of it, but this time, I threw myself into it totally, as I had with many things. Soon after, I was asked to facilitate the classes held at the center due to my vast, preexisting background with other similar teachings. It was destiny unfolding itself.

Very quickly, my class grew, and I continued on the journey that had guided me the whole time by allowing that inner voice, which I had listened to only partially before, to guide me totally. My class grew so large that the facilitator I was substituting for started to take notice and, in my view, was threatened by the growing popularity. Three years into my teaching at the center, he canceled my class. I found this to be a difficult but handy occurrence. I also met my future wife, Lori, the week that class was canceled.

I felt destiny move in. I began teaching my class in a fitness studio and a friend's clothing store. I called my classes *Satsang*, following the lineage of teaching I learned in India. I combined the traditional teachings with *A Course in Miracles*, which had been, in many ways, a missing key in my journey. When I discovered the *Course*, it was as though I had learned from that Voice before, like somehow it was familiar, and I had now come back to it once again. It made perfect sense to me, especially with my background of nonduality from India, which I had begun over a decade before.

Lori, my future wife, eventually started facilitating breathwork at Satsang once a month. I ran the class weekly and by donation because I wanted everyone to have access to the teaching. My classes went on for nearly eight years, during which time thousands of people had attended. This experience brought me to the next part of my journey: becoming a transformational trainer.

While I was teaching, I was involved in small side jobs to make money, which included working for a mobile media company in which I was committed to being successful. When the class at the healing center had been canceled, one of my students had given me the number of another teacher who had taught at the center years earlier whose class had also been canceled. I called him out of the blue, but we didn't meet until nearly a year and half later, when I went to talk to him about the mobile media company I was involved in.

At the time, I was deep in my spiritual journey. I had renewed my passion not only for traveling to India but also for participating in shamanic practices. I was doing ceremonies with shamans from North and South America, while still being deep into meditation, breathwork, yoga, *A Course in Miracles*, and weekly teachings.

During our meeting, this man told me about a program called Gratitude Training. I immediately signed up for it because I felt that patterns in my life regarding money and relationships seemed to be operating on autopilot, no matter how much work I did on myself. The moment I heard that this training was a vehicle for uprooting unconscious patterns, I was totally in. That was the week of my thirty-third birthday.

∞

I was perfectly ready for this huge transformation. The training was life changing, and it was completely evident to me that I was in the right place. Very quickly, I was invited to intern to become a trainer, which took me through three years of intense work on myself and continuously being in the Gratitude Trainings. I was invited to Mexico City to learn from brilliant Master Trainers who were pioneers in the work. The beauty for me was that this is what I had been learning for so many years in all of my reading and travels. I felt renewed and so alive. In many ways, I felt like I was reconciling my childhood experiences and coming back to the place of wonder and joy that had always been present, but not in the way it had been early on in my life.

This was the time when I integrated much of what is written in this book for myself. The trainings were the perfect place for me to bring out these teachings to a large number of people and transform their lives quickly—within a few days, usually. I became the first person to become a trainer who had actually done the Gratitude Training, and rather quickly, I became one of the directors of the company. At the same time, I continued to passionately teach what I learned in India and *A Course in Miracles* to all of the people training to become trainers themselves, as well as to all of the decisions-makers and staff of the Gratitude Trainings.

∞

Never in my wildest dreams could I have imagined where this journey would take me. I married Lori, and we currently live happily together in Florida. I am in trainings thirty-six weekends a year, and I teach and consult privately during the week. The platform is unbelievable, and I am so deeply honored and humbled that this is my calling and destiny. What happened is a merging of what I thought I wanted in the early years and my spiritual journey. They used to be separate, as if my journey were just a passionate hobby. Now, there is no separation. It is what I live and breathe each day. I have come across countless teachers and teachings, from gurus to shamans, trainers, and healers. All of my skills of learning and memory have come in handy in being able to assimilate the teachings and land it for people from all walks of life.

This is an opening for you to learn what has taken me years to notice for myself. I offer you these writings from a humble fellow seeker on the path of life that they may be a glimpse of your own Light and a reminder to yourself of what you are. May you also return to wonder and joy.

HONING IN

When most people start on any path of what might be called Truth or Awakening, they begin by trying to hone in on finding God, Self, or something like that. Their focus is one pointed, in search of, as though they are fishing, honing in on finding fish, and in many cases the perfect fish. The perfect fish can be the perfect job, the perfect partner, the perfect "Truth." What naturally happens is, along the way, things that don't seem to be in line with that are rejected and discarded. It can be as simple as discarding our emotions or as complicated as discarding people we love that we feel don't fit into what we think is in accordance with what we are searching for.

Then, after much searching, there comes a time when we reverse that, and rather than honing in on something, we start expanding outward to include *all* of it as God, or at least all of it as a possibility of showing us God. If *God* is a weird word for us, then we can substitute it with Source, Higher Power, Universal Love, etc. The point is to connect with that which is the substratum of life itself. In this analogy, it would be similar to taking our focus off finding the perfect fish, and then placing our focus on the entire ocean itself. The ocean can be seen, not just by searching for fish, but also by every encounter along the way to finding them.

In the beginning, the path toward Truth is very much about exclusion, about differentiating between and separating out what seems to fit in with our idea of truth and what doesn't. When it shifts, everything is seen as an opportunity for inclusion, an opportunity to be shown one's Self. This means embracing all aspects of myself on the journey, not just what I want to embrace. My emotions of love and also my emotions of fear. All of it is perfect. Most people simplify this into the idea that because it is all perfect or it is all One, that "anything goes" and therefore they can now let go of personal ethics and boundaries. As an extreme example, I cheat on my wife because of some inner struggle or inner compulsion, and then try to explain that it's all perfect. It is on an absolute level, but clearly it is an error on a personal level. Some people, in embracing their darkness as an aspect of themselves—which it is—indulge in it, play with it, and get thrills from it.

I live by the practice of forgiveness, and I believe, in the end, it is really the only path. To forgive all of the "figures in the dream" of my life and to see them as all harmless doesn't mean I put others or myself in harmful situations to prove the ultimate neutrality of things. There is a paradox here of developing our discerning awareness. Everything is ultimately for our own awakening, and we begin to discern what gets us closer to awakening and what takes us away from it, even though *everything* can be a means of forgiveness and awakening.

When awakening is our goal, life becomes, very simply, about extending love and forgiveness and, in many ways, cleaning up our own life and compulsions, and facing the "not-so-pretty stuff" in our relationships. All of this can be used to facilitate forgiveness. So, on one end, everything in our lives can take us toward awakening, and on the other end, we use discernment in choosing what we give our attention to and where we place our energy. We hone in and expand outward at the same time.

THE BODY

For most people, the human body is a source of struggle. We live in a society where we both glorify and hate the body. It seems to be a paradox that even the most "beautiful" and most "perfect-looking" person in the current fashionable trend of the world would probably admit that, deep down, their body doesn't truly fulfill them.

One way of seeing the body is as a beautiful computer-like system that seems to work with an intricacy beyond comprehension, and another way of seeing the body is not much more than an aging apparatus made up of earth, water, and space.

Consider for a moment that time is relative and that everything we see has already happened—from the first nanosecond when time began within the first moments of the universe to what's happening right now. Millions of light years away, events that happened millions of years ago on Earth would appear to be happening today. For instance, if we went far enough into space and looked at Earth, we would still see dinosaurs. Some of the stars we see from Earth have already burned out. So from a certain vantage point, what we are looking at has already passed, has already happened. What if everything that has form is already gone by the time we perceive it? Science calls this the split second delay—everything we see has already passed. That would mean that the body as we perceive it is not really there, that it has already passed.

We all have an experience of the body being here and now, and I am not suggesting we pretend it isn't here so that we have an excuse to abuse it, neglect it, or attack it. (Like a car, we should change the oil and take care of it, but that does not mean we mistake our body for who we are.) Instead, we can each see the body in a new light. The body is the "meat suit" for this journey; it is a device for experiencing what we choose to experience. It is a useful tool while we think we are here. So I take care of my body—I put bandages on its cuts, exercise it, and make sure it gets enough sleep, but that doesn't mean I *am* it.

It would be limiting to suggest you are only that hunk of meat hurtling through space, born to get old and to die. That is the view of the world. This is not what I am suggesting. Rather, I am suggesting that the body is our "digital self," or, as my wife likes to call it, our "Avatar," that I say is "me." The way the world has it, we view our body and see other people's bodies a certain way. It appears we are all separate because of this. So much seriousness comes from what we think we are as a body, how we picture ourselves in our mind, and how others view our "meat suit."

We aren't a body made of the elements of earth, water, and air, but rather we have a body made up of those elements, which is like a shoe we wear for a little while and then take off when we have no more use for it.

∞

CLEAR SPACE

I am moved by what becomes possible for people when they have a clear picture of how they respond and react to life. When they can see it clearly and trust the moment, they can let go of a lifetime of negative thinking. Now, for me as a facilitator, the task becomes how to create the space for this to occur.

What I have discovered is that, to the extent that I can be clear of reacting to them, I can create a space of trust that for my students becomes a safe place to discover. Now if they somehow draw me into an argument—what I would call getting "tagged"—that leads me to be reactive rather than neutral toward them; it diminishes their ability to trust me and impacts the safety of the space. I notice that a teacher can fall short, no matter what their skill set, by thinking they are above a student or by getting frustrated or defensive. This can cause anyone to fall short because the context or space that someone is in will determine the effectiveness of their communication. So much is delivered through the being-ness of a communicator.

So it's my being neutral that creates the clearest mirror for my students to see how they react and respond in life. This comes from their ability to respond to what the moment is bringing and trust themselves to do so—that is, if they have a commitment to discovering this. If they don't, then that will be on them. Now, if I translate that to my life, this means I must be open to the possibilities that the moment may bring forth. I trust in my ability to respond to whatever shows up from a space clear of reaction.

Being a "clearing" in whatever situation I encounter begins with me *experiencing my experience.* When I say "clearing," I mean a space to bring something forth in life. When I don't resist and give everything in life its own place to be, a release manifests as a result. The release is a shift, and with the shift comes a feeling of lightness and openness. The space is clear.

What counters my ability to be light and open—to be a clearing—is my inability to step away from my interpretations of the moment, my inability to surrender my idea of what this experience should be for me. I can't surrender to my experience with all of my beliefs standing in the way of what should or shouldn't be. When I experience my experience, I am allowing it to be what it is; I do this so that something new can show up that wouldn't show up if I were in opposition to the experience itself. By allowing it to be and surrendering rather than being resistant, a space naturally opens up to bring forth something new. When I am clear of what was and accepting of what is, I can then create what will be.

FORGIVENESS

Forgiveness is the key to experiencing freedom and having a joyous life. It is the closest I can get to experiencing Heaven here. The kind of forgiveness I'm talking about is the willingness to recognize that I made it all up. I don't really see the world; I see my picture of it projected outward. In the end, I forgive myself for conjuring up an image of life and of my brothers and sisters that is anything but love. To use this life for something other than the expression of love and peace is a sacrifice, and it's a deep, dark one.

When I see the light, I recognize that I am giving everything I see all of the meaning it has for me. So there really isn't "someone out there" whose actions I am forgiving. It's not about my making what I think they did real and then forgiving that. The very essence of forgiveness is not giving perceived wrongdoings any reality in the first place. It doesn't mean I wouldn't feel and experience a whole range of emotions in life, but I could use all of them for the same purpose: to give me an opportunity to awaken to life's perfection.

When I am willing, for a moment, to surrender the

way I perceive something and recognize that I see it that way because *I* say it is that way, not necessarily because it *is* that way, I am in a space to forgive it. That is what *forgiveness* means. When I am willing to "give forth" the way I see something, a new way can be recognized, a way that sees the innocence in all of life and realizes that I can only be hurt by *my* own thoughts.

The beautiful mirror I have is in my relationships because my willingness to see all of my relationships with forgiveness ultimately determines my peace of mind. Relationships bring up all of my own projections that, when looked at, can reveal my conversations and narratives about life and myself. Whenever I harbor attack thoughts toward another, it is like offering someone poison and then drinking it myself. Like sitting in the prison guarding the one I put in prison, we are both stuck because I must watch them and make sure they stay in the cell I have put them in.

Forgiveness erases all of that through the recognition that the past is past, and the only truth of it is that it isn't the present. It is gone. In this present, I am always free. That's forgiveness. I realize that I wouldn't give someone any response that isn't a fit response for myself because my responses are mirrored back onto me as well. Whatever I give, I receive, and forgiveness makes sure that what I receive is always peace. There isn't anything else to get.

THE EXPERIENCE
OF LOVE AND FEAR

Recently, someone shared with me that they were frustrated and angry. They were attempting to talk themselves out of their frustration and anger by telling me how good they had it. They had all of the basic necessities in life, compared to others who were "less fortunate." As if seeing it that way would make them feel better, they attempted to soothe their frustration by observing that there was so much bad happening in the world, and after all, they had it easy. They also shared with me how that didn't really help them—as I see it, there is a reason that such thinking doesn't work.

Reminding ourselves that we are somehow elevated over those who suffer more than us doesn't alleviate the suffering in this moment, this experience. Such relief requires a radical shift in the way we see our lives and the world. This takes first recognizing the meaning that we assign to everything. It is the mind that we are all on a journey to master. I am reminded of an old quote by the Indian Master Ramana Maharshi, who said, "The mind is everything. It can make a heaven out of hell and a hell out of heaven."

There is plenty of evidence demonstrating that this is the case. Time and time again, we are shown people who are in some of the worst circumstances we can imagine, and they are able to shift their minds. They can do this because there are only two systems of thought. On one hand, my mind is capable of experiencing things like unity, love, freedom, and peace. On the other hand, my mind is capable of experiencing fear, anger, depression, and doubt. The real power in life doesn't come from controlling the factors in our life that are "out there" and thinking that, by controlling them, we will feel good, safe, and protected. In fact, no one knows what the next moment is going to bring; it's a surprise for everyone.

The reason we attempt to control our circumstances and what we think is happening to us is that we think events and circumstances are what cause our experiences. What most human beings fail to see is that we are the ones generating our experiences through our beliefs and perceptions. We all have been deeply programmed to believe that what is happening to us causes our emotions and our reactions, but upon further investigation, this simply isn't the case. It is *always* our beliefs, our stories, and our interpretations around events that cause our discomfort.

The power comes in being able to see this clearly and to interrupt it when we find ourselves in reaction to events, thinking it is the event that caused the discomfort. This is not necessarily easy because of all the hidden thoughts and perceptions people have that are based on the choice of fear, but it is extremely simple. Humans believe that choosing separation and fear actually offers strength and safety. Being weakened already by their beliefs from the past, people buy in to the belief that survival is really the only way, that scarcity is the way that it is, so they choose survival and scarcity as if that somehow protects them.

Whenever we are standing in fear, it's always about our own survival as a separate identity, as a separate being. That's why so many people who seem to have so much from the world's point of view still experience fear and separation. In fact, very often, human beings react to everyday things as if they were a matter of life and death.

That brings me to the point: The only outcome we should ever ask for and want in any situation is the outcome of unity, love, and abundance. It is accessible in every moment, but as I said, it is not always easy to see. There are no quick fixes because our beliefs about what everything is and what it means are so ingrained in us.

We can learn how to interrupt fear and choose love like we are planting a garden. This comes from learning to choose, in every moment, to plants seeds that will continually bear fruit into our future. We recognize that it is a journey of learning to shift from imprisonment into freedom. I would call that shift a miracle because it gives us the opportunity to extend that choice out to the world. It is in that extension that I am truly rich because of how I can see life, not because of how I can control life. My wealth comes from what I already am, not from what I can possess as a separate being in an attempt to survive.

ACCEPTANCE

In looking at what we as human beings have done to one another and ourselves over the years, it can feel deeply disheartening to be human. There have been so many dark aspects of humanity that we are connected to on a conscious and often unconscious level. On the flip side, many teachings have come along that speak of something higher than this "dark cave" of humanity, something that can rescue us from it. Be it religion, philosophy, practices, or penances, all of it aims to explain the root cause of human suffering and find a way out of it.

There is a shadow side in each of us, as well as a side that reflects light, and all human beings have experienced both. Even after hearing about the possibility of enlightenment, liberation, or salvation, no one wakes up and lives happily ever after. I can see it in myself when I am honest. I have been around many so-called enlightened or realized beings, people who promised a road to freedom while they themselves were still subject to this dualistic nature of life. As amazing as I can say my life is—full of freedom, love, abundance, devotion, miracles, and awakening—I still see myself as subject to the temptation of forgetting who I really am.

One of the traps we fall into is that we seek to alleviate the pain and suffering in our own lives with only that which is pleasurable or desirable. So when we experience fear, doubt, or suffering, these feelings become an extra layer of beating ourselves up, of criticism, of disappointment. We have tasted of something "more" or "better," and we want that all the time. The curious thing is that resistance and beating ourselves up for not experiencing what we feel like we should be experiencing in any given moment keeps that negative experience in place.

The miracle of shifting my perception begins with an acceptance of my humanness and what I have generated in this moment. That way there is no war or resistance against what is and what I am experiencing. Fighting against something keeps it in place; what I resist persists. Now, I am not suggesting that we like what is always happening to us. I am suggesting that, in accepting it, we are able to see it from a different vantage point. In accepting both the light and what we perceive as darkness that is around us, we open up a space of accepting both the light and the perceived darkness that is happening within us. That doesn't mean we go out and punch someone who cuts us in line and say, "I am embracing the dark part of myself," but we do realize that we all have the same element in our mind, a darkness, that can push someone to an extreme act of violence.

Resistance to fear and suffering generates fear and suffering. It takes incredible sensitivity and vulnerability to be open to the entire human experience, others and ourselves, and to respond with love to all of it. That creates a space in which we can see and accept that we are on the same level of humanness as everyone else. There is no need to walk around as though we are elevated or superior to others—like we accessed this higher dimension that others can only access if they are lucky. If there is one thing I am certain of, it is that we are all cut from the same cloth. Every teacher and everyone who has ever walked the planet in a body has experienced their own humanness, as well as their own divinity.

Everyone has glimpses of light, of awakening. Whether they are conscious of it or remember it is another story. The problem is that, once we experience the light, most people want to act like they experience it all the time, as though they have achieved this state that others can only hope for. I am calling bluff on that because everyone is on a journey and we are all walking on the path together, walking on our way home. Where you are on the path in this moment doesn't even matter. What matters is that you are on a journey that is continually shifting with possibility and wonder if you are willing to see it . . . and accept it.

MIND ALTAR

All events, circumstances, and experiences are neutral, in and of themselves. They mean only what each person says they mean. That's why someone can experience an event that is similar to another person's experience and derive a completely different interpretation from it. Something as traumatic as physical abuse can hurt one person for the rest of their life and influence all of their relationship choices and how they view themselves, while another person could go through a perceivably worse abuse and consider it their greatest blessing, one that makes them stronger and becomes a source of great learning in them. The event itself is neutral, but how one thinks about the event is *never* neutral because it will shape how they see their life and themselves afterward.

My thoughts aren't neutral because they are constantly generating my experience. Even though what my thoughts tell me may not even be true, I will experience it as true. That's why what I think on a daily basis is so crucial. It shapes everything. A gift that I have discovered is that whenever my mind goes to a fearful thought, there is always an opportunity to change my mind, to shift how I see life, the world, and myself. That shift feels miraculous because, however deeply entrenched my thinking is in fear, scarcity, loneliness, or suffering, when it shifts into love, abundance, connection, and peace, it doesn't even matter what is happening outside me. It doesn't even matter if anything has changed; the moment I change the way I see it, my experience naturally changes. This creates a space where change in circumstances and situations can occur, even if it doesn't happen quickly.

Consistently being mindful of the meaning and interpretations that I bring to events in my life puts me, the perceiver, in a space of power to manifest a life that is congruent with the way I am thinking. Everyone is manifesting a life congruent to the way they are thinking already, but most people are completely unaware of this process. It goes unnoticed. It's for most people on autopilot. That's why it is so important to be aware of our meaning about life, the stories we tell ourselves about who we are, who others are, and how the world is. To be mindful and aware of how we react to things, and what we think, say, and do day in and day out. These thoughts and stories generate what we say and ultimately believe is possible in any given moment. The perceived benefit from our stories and interpretations can show up in various ways, such as being right about how we see something and making others wrong so we can feel justified. Attention, sympathy, avoiding risk and intimacy, control, looking good—all of these are clever goodies we hope to attain with the stories we tell ourselves. We think that events cause our reaction, when it is clearly the beliefs we have about the events that cause our reaction.

If the mind itself were compared to an altar, then it serves us best to be very conscious of what beliefs, stories, and meaning we place on that altar.

CREATING LIFE

It is fascinating to watch human beings create their lives. Why do some people seem to flow with it, while others do not? Why do some experience the universe working in their favor, when for others it seems to be working against them?

When we observe nature, it can provide answers for why specific things show up in certain environments. Whatever shows up in an environment is directly aligned with the environment itself. If something doesn't match up to the environment's frequency or energy, then by law, that something can't show up in that environment. I use an example frequently that palm trees do not grow in New Jersey. They grow in Florida because that is the right environment for them, the right space. The environment that I am as a human being directs what shows up in that space for me. Whatever I want to create, I need to be the correct environment for it to grow in. The space that I am is directly connected to my thinking, my ways of being that result from that thinking, my actions, my habits, etc. Now the clearer I am as a space, the more it's possible for what I want to grow to show up. As

43

an example, I cannot create a loving marriage by being angry and righteous. It doesn't work.

This formula sounds pretty simple, but it's not so easy to implement because there are so many defenses, grievances, and reactions that get in the way of being that clear space. It gets in the way of us experiencing abundance, which is what we truly want to show up, whether we realize it or not. Ironically, this desire leads us to want *things* in life to be a certain way because we think this will help us experience abundance. That's the only reason people want things such as money and relationships—for the experience they think those things will bring them.

What is showing up in my life is a reflection of the space or environment that I am as a human being. The beauty of this is that if something is showing up in front of me that I don't feel is in alignment with my vision of how I want to live my life, I can see it as a beautiful pointer to my underlying automatic beliefs, like fear and scarcity. I get to see it and ultimately let it go so that what I truly want will show up. Fear and scarcity will *not* attract to me what I truly want. That is obvious.

I see many people focus on what is showing up in their lives like they don't know why it is there. Knowing why doesn't always happen right away, although it can, but it is usually an unfolding or a process that can reveal to us the depths of our own mind, including all the pockets of lack, guilt, and shame we hold within us. Most of the time, human beings don't notice this. One of the powers of the mind is to make up pictures, meanings, and stories, and then totally forget that it, the mind, has done so.

In my teachings, I often speak of a dream in which a lion chases me to demonstrate this trick of the mind. When the lion chases me, I run like hell, even though I dreamed up the lion and forgot that I did. Why would we think that when we wake up that same mind isn't doing the same thing in our waking state—creating make-believe pictures from which we want to run like hell?

I know that whatever shows up in my life is there because I am the space and environment for it. I am the one who is creating and observing everything I see and experience in my waking state, which provides me with a profoundly effective way to interact with life. It creates a powerful place of what I would call forgiveness, the "giving forth" of all the pictures, judgments, and beliefs that don't support what we ultimately want, which is the experience of freedom and love. The awareness that we are doing this is the first step. Taking action is the next. It's important to really see the trick of the mind beneath it all.

People often sell out their dreams to hold on to their underlying self-limiting beliefs. They would rather be right about those beliefs than actually create the life they say they want. The life they say they want may not be as difficult to create as they are currently experiencing and thinking it will be. All the inner narratives steeped in fear and scarcity are what make achieving the desired results difficult. It is the water we swim in, scarcity. When we pull away all the layers of this, it's a simple observation that most people would prefer different outcomes for many of the results they are currently producing in life. Most people's results are coming from continually operating old, deeply entrenched programs of fear. Abundance cannot be created in this environment.

Recognizing this, my job becomes to uproot all of those places within myself where fear and scarcity have made their roots; to live my life from a vision with a powerful narrative that confronts my self-limiting beliefs; to pursue all of the dark spots in my mind that I put in the way of the life I say that I am committed to; and to confront those places where I am selling myself a fear-based, self-limiting story because it seems to be easier than to face what frightens me.

This could be said to be each person's challenge and opportunity in life: to be the environment that is aligned with what they say they want to create. How we see this knowledge—the knowledge that the space we are creates our life—and what we do with it determines what shows up for us.

DEFENSIVENESS

Human beings react in their minds as if they are being attacked in their bodies and continually do so every day. There must be some identification with the body for someone to respond to an outside event or situation so strongly that they actually feel like their body is being threatened, when it isn't. Whenever I get angry or afraid, that is the experience I have in my body. It shows up in the body like it is happening *to* the body, even though it always starts in the mind as a thought.

The question I ponder is, with all of the clever strategies or defenses that human beings come up with to protect themselves from the feeling of loss, suffering, and conflict, what exactly are we attempting to protect? All of these strategies are meant to protect a picture in my own mind that somehow seems to be threatened and that I need to defend to "save myself." The defense may be the need to look good or needing to control life in a certain way. It could be staying safe and not risking, staying comfortable. As human beings, we literally operate like there's is a force "out there" that is constantly trying to rob our "kingdom" of peace, joy, and freedom. What if there was no strength in any of the complicated defenses that we set up in our minds? What if the real strength lies in peace and defenselessness?

Now, most people will go right to "it's a cold world out there" or "you can't trust people enough to be entirely without defenses." We can still have strategies for living, such as clear agreements and request for boundaries in our relationships. I'm not talking about what we do or don't do, as much as I am talking about where we are coming from in our hearts and minds while we are interacting with the world. If something is happening to us physically or in our space that may be harmful, we should absolutely do our best to return ourselves and our space to safety. I am talking about something different than that, the constant battle that human beings go through in their minds that has them create defenses that stem from fear. Real strength is found in gentleness and defenselessness.

The moment I need to defend a belief I have of myself or attack another because of their own belief, I have already attacked myself first. I have declared myself weak by believing I would even need defense or by attacking another as a way of boosting my own self-image. All attacks are generated from a belief in weakness. That's why the wars rage on and scarcity seems to be the environment of this planet. We can actually see it operate in our own mind.

What might be possible if we let go of our own internal war and operate from defenselessness, knowing that it is strength? It would take great courage to do this because we would literally be going against everything we have been taught and everything we see happening in the world. The beauty of it is that as we begin to do this with more and more seemingly threatening situations as they arise, we start to see the strength in it. The strength doesn't come from defensiveness, but rather its opposite. Our buttons are no longer pushed, and if they are, we are able to shift off it quicker and easier. It's really a matter of recognizing what it is we actually want and what will get us there. Defenses such as anger and fear don't give us what we want. In fact, they give us the opposite. Surrender and love do give us what we want because they are strong, and ultimately give us what it is we are looking for, in our life and in the world.

ASSESSMENTS

I had always thought that if I was going to let the past go, forgive, and see someone as new in this moment, I needed to throw out all of my discernment and assessments. To see the divine in someone meant that I had no judgments—on that I was clear—but I started to ask a fundamental question: Is there a distinction between judging or condemning someone in my mind and actually assessing how they operate in life, what they are about, and how they live their journey?

I realize there is a paradox here. Each person is nothing less than everything—God, Spirit, whatever you would like to call it. There is also within each person a part of their mind that is steeped in separation, suffering, loss, and fear. Each of us has a choice between those two aspects of mind. Regardless of what anyone chooses, they are still perfect, whole, complete beings, yet it is clear that some people are so lost in fear that they don't wish themselves and others well. To them, I can only offer forgiveness, but that doesn't mean I invite them over to my house for holiday dinner.

We do need to assess everything, even to cross the

street in this world, and yet condemnation of someone hurts *me*, the one condemning that person. That reveals my own hurt, my own wounds in life. Most people collapse this by thinking that to be spiritual or loving, they must accept everything—"anything goes"—without standing up for what they truly believe is ethical, right-minded, and loving.

Now, someone might use that as a justification for their own righteousness, which isn't what I am suggesting. I am suggesting that we can be so deeply compassionate and loving with others and ourselves that we can speak up and disagree with the hurtful things they do to themselves and the world around them. We create clear boundaries for others and ourselves *as* an expression of love. This challenges the whole idea that everything is perfect. Yes, it is all perfect, and yet I would hardly say that a psychotherapist sleeping with their patient is perfect. Rather, they reveal that everyone is acting in perfect integrity with their beliefs and values, even though in those situations they will most likely be creating pain.

That being said, the question becomes: How can I be a space of forgiveness and take a powerful stand for what I assess to be good, loving, and compassionate? That is a question I say we all must ask ourselves, and we must each come to a conclusion that produces love and goodness in the world.

CLEANING UP

When we dive deeper into uncovering our Self, past our identities and pictures of who we think we are, some of the thrills that once got us "high" often don't work anymore. There is a difference between wanting to get "high" on experience and seeing that, ultimately, no experience can give us the recognition of the completion we so desperately seek.

We seek experiences to give us a certain sense and recognition of the picture of our self that we cling to. Human beings are constantly being taught that more is better, and this generates a compulsion toward seeking thrills and acquiring objects or experiences that add to the idea of ourselves. These may include fame, money, sex, and so on. There is a power that comes from letting go of that because, when we do, we start to recognize ourselves as being beyond any experience, beyond any thought or emotion. That which we are, as awareness earlier than any experience, is where our power and our completion resides.

This is why so many mystics and saints have withdrawn themselves from the world. While I don't think that outwardly turning away from the world (living in a cave, for instance) is necessary, I do feel it needs to be done inwardly. That's how we clean up our game.

When I say, "clean up our game," I mean looking into those places within ourselves where we seek thrills and crave certain experiences and ultimately turn away from them in favor of a deeper experience of who we truly are. When we withdraw from those places inside us, we naturally generate a certain energy through discipline of our thoughts and actions. This ability to generate energy is very often overlooked because most people think that doing whatever they want, whenever they want, and however they want constitutes freedom. The irony is that the opposite is true.

When we allow a vision of awakening to our inherent completeness guide us, we can seek to open that up, rather than collecting more experiences to reinforce an identity of ourselves. It comes down to dedicating our lives to awakening who we really are, not who we perceive ourselves to be. That comes from devoting our lives to seeking, and using all things that come to us—thoughts, feelings, and experiences—as the ground for that discovery. In seeing that, we clean up our lives and let go of anything that becomes a distraction.

There are many ways to take me closer to this recognition, and when I choose to be honest with myself, I see that some things, like compulsion and specific thrills, distract me and take me away from who I really am. Getting closer to seeing who I truly am takes honesty because the world can be such a seductive distraction to this recognition. Our compulsions can show us where we are distracted, where we are caught. The question to ask is: "Do I *need* this? Will I feel complete without it?" If the answer is no, that is a great place to start cleaning up. Someone who recognizes their wholeness and completion needs nothing in this world to fill them up. Ultimately, we realize that nothing in this world can add to us, and nothing in this world can take away from us. We are whole.

A TRAP

One of the traps I see in spiritual modalities is that those who adopt a specific path can become cold or insensitive to the suffering of others. It becomes easy to offer up a spiritual concept or "enlightened" jargon when we are confronted with someone else's fear, pain, or grief. (The ironic thing is that we don't just as easily do the same when our own struggles arise.)

To be sensitive to the suffering of another being, we don't need to join them in their "dark night." To be the space of healing for someone requires a sensitivity and compassion that can only come from understanding our own pain and what the cause of all pain is: beliefs ingrained in our minds about life, who we say we are, and what everything means. Although it only takes an instant to transform these beliefs, it may take some time to get to that place. A lot of people go wandering around, hearing from teachers and so-called gurus that all you need to do is change your mind. While that is correct—all it takes is a change of mind—the process, I have found, is very much like creating a garden. Soil needs to be tilled, seeds planted, watering done consistently, and so on. It's wishful thinking to suggest that a garden blooms in a moment. We have to plant the seeds of happiness and joy, and they will sprout in their own time.

It's the same with so-called transformational work. So many people walk around like they have "gotten" it and can't understand why others don't "get" it, and that makes them insensitive to the pain and suffering of those who don't "get" it. Transformation requires a deeper understanding that this process of atonement, or awakening, involves subtle processes on so many levels that it would be arrogant to assume where someone else is on their journey or to take pride in where we are on ours.

The ultimate recognition is that there isn't a "person" there to even claim "getting" it for themselves or superiority over others who are less fortunate because they haven't "gotten" it. The whole idea that "I get it" and "others don't" is to miss the whole point of what awakening or enlightenment is. It simply dresses up our self-identification in pretty, more "spiritual" clothes. This realization brings us to the eternal, present moment where, instead of even being transformed, we can create in ourselves a space of love and compassion where transformation and healing can occur. The result is a genuine humility and sensitivity to the pain of others, not an elevation and superiority over them for what we have "accomplished" and they have not that somehow makes us better and puts us beyond all of that in life.

We are all here learning, and as Ram Dass says, "We're all just walking each other home." Superiority on the path, whether it is on the way up the mountain or at the top, is a trap that, very often, is harder to see in ourselves at that point on our journey than it would have been when we were at the bottom just starting our climb.

THE EARNEST JOURNEY

The greatest remedy I have found for the suffering that human beings go through is to recognize they are on a journey, a hero's journey of awakening that takes each of us through the maze of our own conscious and unconscious mind. The moment I do that, everything that shows up in my life becomes a vehicle or mirror to show me myself.

In the beginning, it is like I am trying to make out the figures on a wall in a dark room with a flashlight that can barely give off any light. The images are faint and seem vague and unclear. This moment can discourage most people from the journey itself. A sincere, earnest willingness to discover is the most important tool for making clear what is being projected on the wall. I have found that the whole universe bends to earnestness.

Through earnest discovery, I am able to finally make out the images on the wall in the dark room of my mind. They become distinct. I now understand where those fears came from, where that anger and doubt came from. The way I set up the whole game of my life becomes clear. Grace begins to enter with my earnestness. Whether it's called "Spirit" or "The Inner Guide," it's as if I realize that I am being guided.

What seems to block that is the world and all of its whispers of *You are separate from all of life; this is reality— you are born and you die, so get as much as you can in between so you can survive.* That voice is so loud for most people that they never follow the call to wake up to the truth of what they are, that they are an eternal expression of life. They never hear it. It's been said, "Many are called but few listen." The way I see it, everyone is called, so make sure your whole life becomes about listening. That is the difference between a life that looks like a chaotic, random set of events all coming from a challenging force that is outside your control and a life that seems like the universe is always working to your advantage.

You are being led as though you are gently flowing down a river. The river is constantly heading in the direction of your own fulfillment and your inherent wholeness. The curious thing about this is that everyone's journey is so unique for them. It's like I start off with a smorgasbord of choices that I get to narrow down to which method or modality will be the "boat" that will take me through the ocean of my life. I have found that all the boats may look different, but all are basically similar. My boat may look like meditation, trainings, breathwork, shamanic rituals, certain inquiries and contemplations, and specific methods and practices. My boat takes me on a journey through these modalities led by my "Inner Guide."

The question is, "Have I surrendered to that Guide? Have I developed myself in such a way that I am able to discern what my Inner Guide is telling me from what my past belief systems are telling me?" Most human beings are not able to differentiate between the two. The journey, then, is diving deep within oneself so you can finally learn to listen and let go of the compulsions, beliefs, righteousness, control, safety, and comfort that are focused on surviving.

As I surrender more and more to that, my experience is that not only do I survive but also that it is impossible for me *not* to. I am constantly thriving. I am being led, and what I am at my core is whole, complete, and free.

COMPLETION

When I look at most spiritual teachings, there is often an underlying theme of getting the world to be the way I want it to be so that my result is a specific experience, whether it is something like finding a loving relationship or making more money. Even those who have beliefs about the afterlife require themselves to experience the world in a specific way while they are here, whether it is to make themselves special or to give them hope for something better (i.e., the concepts of heaven and hell). There are a few teachings that speak about transcendence of this world, not in an afterlife sense but in the sense that everything here is illusory, that nothing here can make me more complete than I am or lessen me in any way.

Ultimately, everything that happens and everything I see is more reflective of me as a seer than it is on what I see or what people consider reality. Ironically, the less attached I am to the desire to make the world look a certain way, the more the world shows up looking the way I would like it to look. There is a paradox inherent in this. The Bible says, "Seek ye first the kingdom of heaven, then all will be added on to you." It doesn't say to "Seek ye first everything you want added onto you, then you will find the kingdom of heaven." That's the difficulty.

In many ways, the world serves as a way for us to avoid seeing the kingdom of heaven. Human beings take whatever they feel they need from the world to fill a gap they believe is within them. I see how I have done that, and whether it is specialness from sex, body image, wealth, power, prestige, or fame, it is all the same at the core. We wouldn't even desire or need any of those things if we are in a state of completion, so there must be a sense of incompleteness present that causes any one of us to seek for them.

If we knew of our inherent completeness, I wonder if any of us would even come to this world of experiencing to constantly chase after things. Life seems to be constant seeking, and for the one that is totally complete, seeking doesn't even make sense. Now that doesn't mean we aren't going to seek here; as I see it, seeking is inherent to the game we call life. The question is, *What am I seeking and why?* Is it to control life and the world or to recognize the impossibility in that? Is it to wake up to a greater sense of self, of knowing and recognizing my own intrinsic wholeness already or to keep chasing and hoping that one day I will feel complete? Those are two diametrically opposed ways of seeing the world. One wants something from the world, and the other brings something to the world. One seeks completion via the things of the world to make bigger or better the picture of oneself. The other is about bringing to the world one's own completion.

My entire journey appears to be a settling into this,

and I can honestly say that my life and world today are more like I would want them to be than I have ever thought I could have it. I have a beautiful marriage and a life of purpose, abundance, and fulfillment. While I go through this dance, I can be fully engaged in it, while also observing it as it all passes by, like clouds in the sky. I am fully engaged in it, and yet at the same time not affected by it—not in terms of my wholeness.

Remember, this is not an excuse to do whatever we want because nothing matters. I want to challenge this way of seeing and invite all of us to go beyond that, to a place where everything that matters is of goodness and wholeness and the expression thereof. I would never want to bring anything else to the world because I would never want anything else to come to me except that: goodness and wholeness. What I give is what I will receive. It is responsibility, in the ultimate sense.

The purpose of the world is that I may see a part of myself in all beings, in all things, and have a genuine desire to impart goodness and love to all things. At the same time, I can be discerning about what fits into my story and which characters I will cast. That doesn't mean I can't extend love to everyone, but there is a difference between grabbing a tea with someone and inviting them to my home for a Sunday dinner. When I see myself and everyone as complete, it ultimately becomes a matter of deciding what moments are best for me to devote my limited time to in this play called life.

Where will I go? What will I do? There is no required way my life needs to look and the most beautiful thing about it is that I can extend my completion and remind others of theirs in the smallest of situations, such as at the gas station, all the way up to the largest situation, as when I'm on stage in front of a crowd of people. The form of the situation doesn't matter. What matters is that I recognize the completion in myself and genuinely seek to remind others of their own as well.

THE WITNESS

We are *It*. As human beings, it is so ingrained in us to identify with worldly things that something so clear and closer than our own breath—the most powerful resource we have—is often overlooked. If I were to ask what the common denominator is in every experience, in every thought, in everything seen and felt, the only answer anyone could give that would be true is "I am."

My body has totally changed since I was a child. My personality, my knowledge, my experiences—they have all changed. Nothing is the same. Nothing is even the same from year to year, day to day, or even moment to moment. The earth is in an entirely different place right now than it was when I started typing this. So everything—time, memory, space, thoughts, feelings, experiences, and so on—has to have a common denominator, and it is always the same; it is inevitably the sense of "I am."

A Course in Miracles says, "I am the light of the world." We are literally the light of the world we perceive; it can't be any other way. If we, the witness, are taken away, then where does the experience of life and the world go? It disappears. There is something very liberating in that and obviously also something very scary in that for most human beings.

We have been conditioned to look everywhere else but within for our worth and identity. We've been taught that we can find our value in collecting things, status, how we look to others, money, sex, and so on. We have all been taught to look everywhere for our value, except in the one place that it already is: where we are looking *from*. This awareness that even allows you to read this book and say, "I agree or I disagree"—that awareness is the most fundamental aspect in all experience. Its obviousness is often overlooked in favor of something supposedly "greater" in the world.

That doesn't mean that being a renunciate for the rest of our days is the answer, but it does mean that we can always remember what is really at play in every moment. Ram Dass spoke about the women in Africa who carry their laundry baskets on their head while they walk, talk, and interact. I am sure they don't have to concentrate on the basket in every moment. They can laugh and talk with one another, but they are aware that the basket is on their head. We can do the same thing by remembering clearly that who we are is not only enough but is actually the light, the source, the foundation of all that we see and witness in our minds, in others, and in the world.

A time will come when we will not look for our worth and our identity in what we see because we will find it in that which is the witness for and witnesses to all of life. In that moment, everything witnessed will be seen like clouds in the sky that create rainy days, beautiful days, wet days, and dry days but never affect or put out the rays of the sun. This experience comes from a general withdrawal of the value that we have placed on things in the world. Most people take up all belief systems and even spiritual practices as a means of getting something, or making their life better than it already is. We chase after pleasure and avoid pain. When we stop for a moment and seek only to recognize the totality of wholeness, and make *that* what we are really after, it becomes obvious that we have been given everything already—that we *are* everything already.

There is lightness and silence in the essence of who we are, beyond words and beyond clinging to the world. It is our true capital, our true gift, and cannot be found because it cannot be lost. When I make *that* what my life is about, what I am really seeking, I naturally see that what I am seeking is what I already am. What I am seeking is where I am seeking from. The witness, the subject, is ultimately what is already whole, and it can never find its wholeness in outer objects. When I turn away from seeking outward and allow that seeking to be inward, the witness reveals itself as the drop of water from the ocean of infinite life.

YEARNINGS

There is a difference between what I want in the world and the deeper yearnings that want to come through me. When I was in business for myself for many years, no matter how much I visualized and was committed to what I thought I wanted, it didn't turn out that way. When the financial markets crashed in 2008, there was a time when I barely had enough money to take care of my basic necessities. I may have been committed to abundance and thought it was going to look a certain way, but what came from all of that crashing down was beyond anything I could imagine—something I couldn't see at the time.

Abundance is here, now, but not in the way I had thought it would show up. There is a powerful observation in this because there was something deeper for me that wanted to come forth, and there was a moment when I remember surrendering to that. That yearning was so deep that I said to myself, "I would be on the street with a begging bowl if that's what I need to live in the vision of what wants to come through me."

Well, I ended up far from begging. In fact, when it

clicked, it was very clear that I was being led, and my greatest strength came in the surrender to that call, that commitment. It was as if all arrows were pointing in the right direction, whereas before they were all pulling me in different directions. The paradox is, when I stopped searching for what I thought I wanted and listened to the inner voice, life showed up in a way greater than I had *thought*. It was as if I didn't know what was in my own best interest. I am grateful that most of what I thought I wanted didn't turn out to be so. I watched the people who seemed to have the most financially, lose the most, and I looked back and felt appreciative to have learned that lesson at a young age and without much damage.

Most of what we want comes from a feeling of lack within ourselves, and when we see that there really is no lack, no gap, then everything that shows up in life is great, but none of it is needed. Nothing is needed for our own freedom because we see that we are already free. I feel this is a key point to manifesting abundance in life: seeing oneself as already abundant, rather than seeking for something to prove that one is abundant. If we are magnets, then when we chase after something, we push it away; even if, at first, we catch it, we can't hold on to it. This underlying feeling of lack will ultimately push everything away from us because abundance cannot coexist with scarcity.

The key is to first see myself whole and complete, lacking nothing. From there, all things can flow through me. I can open my hands to allow it to come through me rather than hold on to it. The holding on is death; the letting go is life, flow. All my searching and vigilance needs to be against seeing any lack in myself, or rather recognizing there is no lack in myself. From there, all things can come to me in the recognition that I have already been given everything of value, which is what I am. My natural inheritance is, itself, perfection. What happens then is that most everything that I once sought and wanted as a separate being is now replaced by a deeper yearning for something that is ultimately greater than myself to come through me.

HOLY RELATIONSHIP

What I consider to be a holy relationship—a space where two people use their relationship as a mirror for their own awakening, recognizing that their awakening is intimately reflected by that relationship, and allow that relationship to become a vehicle for bringing their awakening out into the world—is possible. In intimate relationships, we have the opportunity to work on that with one person. I experience that with my wife, Lori.

I am discovering that an intimate relationship can be the catalyst for bringing holiness to all the other relationships, even the ones with strangers we might encounter on the street. Now, I am not suggesting we bring that stranger home for coffee and dessert, although we may, but I am suggesting that the intimate relationship we call our primary relationship can be the soil for our deepest growth and greatest seeing.

It takes great discipline to use one's primary relationship for such growth. The love that is generated from that growth can be brought to life itself. That doesn't mean we take the love we generate and go share that intimacy with everyone. What I am suggesting is to dive so deep into intimacy with one person, allowing it to shape who you are at such a fundamental level that it radically alters how you see yourself and the world. Through this, you can become the type of being who sees the love within yourself and uses the relationship as an expression of that love. From there, you can extend this out into the world, into life.

Most people don't take their partner's well-being as an indicator of their own. Even when their partner is going through something that is hard, these people believe that struggle has to do with their partner's "work" and not their own. I even see people who think it is good that their partner is in that dark space, that it is good for their partner to struggle working on themselves. The longer one of us stays in the dark space, working on "ourselves" specifically because of something the other has done, the less time we have to give to others and the world. Let's face it: We need healed people on the planet right now, and the more my wife stays in her darkness because of something I am doing or something the relationship is putting her through, the less time we have to go out together and be a light to the world.

I do understand that people in any type of relationship —whether husband and wife, child and parent, or some other dynamic—have stuff to work through. Ultimately, it has nothing to do with one person or the other. Whatever there is to see and work on is deeply intertwined with both of them. There is not "their stuff" and "my stuff"; there is what is showing up with us, whatever our relationship may be. Most people in relationships spend a great deal of time separating what is "mine" from what is "theirs"; there isn't a total surrender into "us." The irony is we have been taught that it is good and healthy to fight and have a sense of separation present in the relationship.

What I am proposing is a new possibility where the purpose of a relationship is to see the holiness that each individual is by seeing the core sameness of each. That is the ultimate purpose of all relationships, and the intimate relationship can be a springboard for seeing this, should we choose to use it for that purpose.

∞

DREAMER
OF THE DREAM

Someone told me today that he noticed that it's as if he is coming from two different places in his life. When he spoke about his experience, he was comparing his life to a dream. (Most of us have heard the analogy that "life is a dream.") What he noticed was that there seemed to be two aspects of dreaming. One aspect was like lucid dreaming so he knew he was dreaming. He could sense and see things before they happened in a space where he himself was authoring the dream. He was calling forth everything in that space to himself as the dreamer of the dream. The other aspect was when he noticed that he was having a "bad day" or things weren't going right; at those times, he said it was as if another force was doing what it wanted in the dream and he was at the mercy of it.

The very nature of what it means to dream is that a dream is illusory. Now it's obvious that when you dream of being in danger, you most likely wake up in a pool of sweat with your heart racing. That doesn't mean you didn't dream up the danger you believed was there. Even though you forgot you dreamed it up and treated it as real does not make it reality. We could say the same thing about our lives.

There are only two places to come from while dreaming. One of them is that you are the dreamer of the dream, and the other is that you are at the mercy of the dream. They bring opposite experiences of dreaming. Keep in mind that both are still dreams, and before we talk about what is beyond dreaming, I believe it is important to first understand that we are dreaming. We can have either a nightmare or, as *A Course in Miracles* calls it, a happy dream.

What is beyond dreaming cannot be understood in dream language or perception. It can only be pointed at, and we can use symbols to speak about it, but ultimately, it is beyond anything we can understand while dreaming. We can see this in our own experience. When I am robbed in my dream, it would make no sense to call the police when I wake up. In fact, that dream is no longer accorded reality when I wake up.

What if it is the same with our lives? If that were the case, I am only concerned with recognizing that I am dreaming and turning it into a happy dream. Now, having a happy dream isn't necessarily about getting the dream the way that I want it to be, but rather about seeing that I am dreaming and realizing that nothing in the dream can ultimately hurt me. I must recognize that I made it all up.

It is only when we forget that we are dreaming that the dream seems to be a force outside us that threatens our sense of freedom and peace. When we remember that we are dreaming, it's like the dream becomes a beautiful dance; we play with dream figures for a little while, realizing deep down that ultimately they can't touch us.

In the end, we can let the final step of going beyond the dream rest in the hands of the One who is beyond time, space, and dreaming. When the moment that is beyond time occurs, you will see for yourself that you are and have always been the ONE who is ultimately beyond any dream.

∞

MEMORY OF EXPERIENCE

The world is a mirage. There is nothing in it that could add to anyone, and nothing in it that could take away from anyone. I don't mean in actual physical form, like "They took my car, so I have less now." I mean what we are at our core cannot be added to or subtracted from. Everything I have ever gotten—all of the praises, successes, thrills, the milestones, all of it—has not added to what I am right now. Some may say it adds to my experience of myself, but that is only through the memory of the past experience. On the flip side, all of the things that hurt me—the fights, the heartbreaks, the deaths, all of it—hasn't taken away anything from what I am right now. If I feel that it has, it again is only through memory of that past experience.

Right now, in this moment, being alive, I have the same capital, the same mechanism, for experiencing as I did when I was a child. With all the "good" things and all of the "bad" things that have happened, I am still the same space of awareness; I haven't changed. I am still there in this moment with the possibility of being present to whatever is showing up.

All experiences, all thoughts, all feelings, everything I have collected, everything that hurt me, all the pride, all of the fear and guilt, all of the power, the fame, the health, the sickness—ALL of it will disappear into dust. None of it will last. It will all pass by like clouds. Everything that comes will go. That is a fact. If we could simply see this and stop chasing after these things, demanding what we see out there to be a certain way, and recognize that even what we label as "bad" is only our view from this moment, a level of acceptance and calm would settle in.

It's like watching a movie. There will be a huge variety of images and moments we will see on the screen. We will laugh at some of it, cry at some of it, be frightened by some of it, and angry with some of it, but does any of it affect us after we walk out of the cinema, except in memory? How is it any different in our life, besides that we say "me" and "mine" about everything? If a neighbor's dog died, I may feel bad for them and send condolences and perhaps even shed a tear with them, but within a short period of time, life would be back to normal. I would let that experience move through me. Now, if it were "my" dog, then all hell could break loose, and it could feel like the heavens have closed in on me and the whole world came crashing down. One could go into a depression for a long time because of that. And the only difference is the attachment of "me" and "mine" to that dog and that experience—the memory is the glue that keeps me attached.

Nothing from the past or the future can affect me, except as a thought. Just as I have made it through all of the experiences up to now, I will also do that to the end of *this* experience of life, of *this* current movie I appear to be in, for *this* brief moment of time on a planet spinning around a star in the middle of nowhere in an enormous universe. Being aware of this, I can breathe and relax.

THREE STATES
OF BEING

There are several basic facts that are fundamental to all human beings. First, everyone is conscious; everyone knows that they exist. If anyone tried to prove otherwise, they would prove their own existence simply by doing so. Second, every human being has a sense of conscious presence—or what I like to call "I am"—and goes through a cycle of waking state, dream state, and deep sleep state, all dependent on this sense of "I am." Without it, these states don't exist.

Now, this aliveness is dependent, it seems, on a body, and the breath as well, which are both vital to all human beings. The body itself is in many ways a "host" to this aliveness, this sense of "I am," and from there, the states of waking, dreaming, and deep sleep are constantly moving about, in some ways like a pendulum. When I am in the dream state, my body is not present to me in the same way as in the waking state, although I can be present to my self, my body, and other bodies. They aren't as "solid," so to speak.

Another interesting characteristic of our consciousness is that the dream state and the waking state are each
experienced as a reality on their own, as an individual
state. For instance, during the dream in which I am being
chased by a lion, I am running for dear life, even though I
am the one dreaming the dream. I imagined both the lion
and myself as the person running from the lion. There is
a sort of hypnosis in which I have forgotten that I am the
one who dreamed it all up. (Unless I am having a lucid
dream, I am not aware that I am dreaming.)

The same can be said in the waking state. Even
though I may be going through something that I experience in the waking state of existence as "serious" and
"real," when I fall asleep and dream, I leave that waking
state altogether. That's not to say I won't have remnants
of it during my dreams. For example, I may dream about
what happened at work today, but what I view as my
reality has shifted, and the interesting thing is that in
deep sleep, all of that is gone. No dreaming, no dreamer,
no waking state and all of its forms—nothing is there. I
am still alive and I still exist, but my lapse in memory and
time makes it seem like some sort of "blank."

Even though there isn't an experience that I can
remember, what is still there? I clearly am alive in it; I can
wake up to someone calling me, or even, in some cases,
wake up a minute before my alarm clock goes off! I know
many people who report that experience, so it is clear we
are still alive; the "I am" flame is still there.

Now there is a possibility that this awareness that
allows us to know we are alive and that everything else is,

is always there, is eternal. I don't mean the "I am Chris" state itself because it is clear that people drop the body, the breath, and the "I am so-and-so" with it, as far as we can see. When we see a corpse, what is left of what once was? I think it is obvious to us that there is a shift to some degree when we leave the body. An element of "I am Chris" goes with it. I can only assert that the space that is here, right now, is omnipresent. This space in which the "I am" arises in is always here. That is all anyone can ever really do when we point at it. The pointer is never it.

Once this "I am" develops like a seed, we all start to tell ourselves certain things about life, through the mechanism of what many call the "mind." That mind tells us what everything is and what it means, and, like the dreamer forgetting he is dreaming and thinking he is in full reality, whatever the mind tells us is true about the world is regarded as reality.

So far, nothing I have written about this has to do with any philosophy or any belief; it's just simple observation. I can say that anything beyond these basic facts that are observable in every human experience is, in fact, a postulation. That doesn't mean it's bad or wrong, but the moment I forget that I am simply telling nice stories about everything and that they are only present in my waking state, and sometimes in my dream state, then I am no different from the dreamer who runs from the lion, forgetting he is dreaming. That means that all beliefs about God, death, enlightenment, light and darkness, right and wrong action, etc., all are made up—nothing more than dream stuff. That isn't good or bad, which are labels we like to apply to what we make up; it simply is what is.

When human beings remember that they are making it all up, they gain a lightness and compassion for others and lose the need to be right about their own beliefs, about the way they think others should or shouldn't be. For some people, to even look at this clearly, to see it in their everyday life and experience can be frightening.

Remember, this isn't about how the dream should or shouldn't be; human beings have the ability at their disposal to set it up any way they like. I am stating that we are *making it all up and totally forgetting that we are doing this.*

When this is clearly understood, it's natural to let go of the need to be something or get something or have the dream be a certain way. It doesn't take away the possibility that we can mold our dream the way we like. In actuality, we have a greater chance to make the dream look a certain way if we can simply recognize that we are dreaming. We become less attached to the dream. We can recognize also that there are ways to have the dream be a pleasant one when we live by purpose, love, and peace. Since we are making it all up, why not make up stuff that works and has us live a happy dream instead of a nightmare? The body itself is put into the proper perspective as being a vessel for the "I am" and for experiencing all that happens while it is here and that it will be laid by when it is complete.

It also puts me in the proper perspective to realize that who I am is the basic factor in *all* I experience, and without my being there as the observer, there is nothing to observe. I am the most important aspect of the dream because without my sense of conscious presence, there is no dream. The awareness of "I am" is the most basic, fundamental point in all that I am experiencing. Without it, this dream of who I think I am is not there. Ultimately, we are already everything of value because we are the dreamer of our dream and recognizing that shifts entirely how our dream is experienced.

THE ROOT CAUSE
OF TROUBLE

Incidents like shootings in the nightclub in Orlando during the summer of 2016, where more than fifty people were murdered and many more were injured, make people think, including myself, *What is the remedy for hate? What is my role in all of this, and how do I bring the world to a higher level of consciousness and conscience?*

There are many layers to a conversation like this. There is the water in which we swim, which is centered on greed. Something in the current environment of the world has people believing in separation and hatred resulting in the haves and have-nots. Part of the conversation regards people who have no conscience—and their ability to entice people with a conscience to abandon it in favor of what seems to be a noble fight. There is also a conversation about war and its ineffectiveness.

The current conflict with terrorism, to me, clearly represents another type of war, one that is being waged inside the hearts of each one of us. Just like terrorism, it is difficult to see within ourselves, and it is also difficult to see within one another. There is a certain law that abides in this world, and whether we want to accept it or not, it still exists. If I take from you so that I can have, we both have lost. That is why there are certain things in this world, things that go against the conscience of each of us, that are fundamentally wrong. It is wrong to rape and murder another human being. The reason it is wrong—or wrong-minded, we can say—is that for someone to do that to another person, they have already lost; they have lost the recognition of the goodness within themselves. Such goodness is experienced when we give love and our hearts to one another. It is lost in our experience when we take from or hurt one another.

I don't believe on an absolute level that goodness is entirely gone, as I believe we are all innocent and whole, as Spirit, as God created us. However, we won't experience ourselves that way when we take from others, when we see ourselves as separate from them or superior to them. That is the root cause of all of the trouble happening on the planet. Some human beings have learned that taking from another is a way to win. It is not. We have to be careful to avoid developing a cynical view of life because of that. Certain people need to be removed from power and certain policies need to be enforced; that is obvious. That is on a level of doing, but on the level of being, which is a distinct paradigm from the level of doing, we each need to look within ourselves to see the war we wage there.

The world is not separate from me; it is all connected. We made terrorism; we made up the world the way that it is. The collective consciousness of humanity generated the world the way it is today. On one level, it's all of us, and on another level, it is the result of individuals acting from conflict. They are acting in accordance with the ego, which is the very base of scarcity and lack, and the idea that winning in life is about "me." What is happening on the planet now, just as it has been for thousand of years, is a result of the ego, the idea that, somehow, we can be separate from the whole.

Ego thrives on war, on taking, on the idea that I can win for me even if you lose. We can easily point out the ego in others without confronting the ego within ourselves. So this, just as with all things that happen in life, can be used to ask ourselves which inner voice we will listen to. Will it be the voice that speaks for me only, that thinks taking is a way to win and conflict is a way to bring peace? Or will we listen to the voice that recognizes that everyone is an essential part of my Self, and that by giving, I receive? One of those voices disregards life and others. The other voice has regard for all and treats all of life with dignity and respect.

Paradoxically, on one level, we can take action to deal with certain individuals who may be upsetting to the whole, and on another level, we can be dignified and have integrity while doing that. Adolf Hitler needed to be dealt with. Even though his ideology was of separation and hatred, we must see that he was a result of our own consciousness as human beings. I am not saying he literally existed because of you and me, but he showed us ourselves, a part of our own mind.

There have been many "Hitlers" over the years, and some are alive right now. There also have been many "Mother Teresas" over the years, and some are also alive right now. We have created the environment where people like them can grow. And since everything is connected, I am a part of the seed of hatred sprouting and I am also part of the seed of love sprouting. All of the good and all of the bad—all of it—is within me.

So the greatest gift I can give to the world is the gift of my own awakening, my own healing. It is why the lesson in *A Course in Miracles* states, "When I am healed, I am not healed alone." We are intimately connected and our mind is joined to the whole. Every dark cornerstone that goes unhealed within us is impacting all of it, just as every time we access the light within us, that also is. The root cause of trouble comes when we forget this and act as though we are independent of life itself. It is impossible that we are separate from life; yet that is how most of humanity is currently operating. The opportunity to shift this lies within each one of us, in each moment.

UNREST

The 2015 Baltimore Protests, which were spurred by the events surrounding the death of Freddie Gray, culminated in riots throughout Baltimore. To most, this may have seemed like an isolated violent uproar based on an incredibly unfortunate event, but this type of unrest is reflective of what is happening on our planet on a global scale.

In attempting to correct the problem, people make the mistake of treating such circumstances as if they exist independent of the overall environment of scarcity that we, as a planet, are operating from. The outcome is similar to that of walking into a bathroom where the faucet is stuck and the sink is overflowing, and instead of pulling the drain plug, we look for the best mop possible and put a team together to mop around the clock, and everything we look at in terms of a solution is all based around mopping. Do we have the right amount of moppers and the best mops? As long as we, as a society and as a world, want to operate from the idea that "more is better for me" and disregard the fact that if I win and others lose, we both lose, we will continue to see problems like Baltimore pop up all over the world.

It doesn't take a rocket scientist to figure out that our food is poisoned because of the same scarcity context. Our banks are lying to the people because of the same context. We fight wars because of the same context. We suppress the opportunity of certain races because of the same context. We glorify profit at all costs, even if it means negatively impacting the lives of some human beings, because of the same context.

Until humanity wakes up to the fact that no one is really winning until *everyone* is winning, then Baltimore is simply the next war on the docket. Mopping up the floor doesn't work. The shift has to happen at a more fundamental level, which is at the level of our consciousness as human beings. When that shift occurs, we can pull the plug because the scarcity context from which we operate exists only in our minds. We could feed everyone on the planet right now, but we won't because of the scarcity we believe in.

True, lasting change has to happen at a fundamental level, and there is nothing more fundamental than our thinking. It has gotten us into this situation, and, as Albert Einstein said, "We cannot solve our problems with the same thinking we used when we created them." There has to be a fundamental change in mind. That means it starts with *me*.

The beautiful thing about the mind is that one person can shift the minds and consciousness of many. We get to change our minds and think from the context of abundance in our own life, and then take action from that place. That action may mean healing a "war" in one's own family. It may mean donating one's time and money to someone in need. It may mean speaking up to government officials and creating a movement. What the action is won't matter as much as the mind from which the action stems. We must shift from a context of lack to one of abundance, and then we will realize that we have enough, that we are enough, and that truly winning means we all are winning—all races, all religions, all genders. Until we focus on this, then whatever Band-Aids we attempt to put on the problem will ultimately fail.

It is time for a revolution of the mind on a grand scale and for *everyone* to wake up. If we would continue as a species on earth, then it will take a radical shift from scarcity to abundance—from *me* to *we*—so that we understand that no one is winning unless everyone is.

BEGINNINGS, ENDINGS, AND IN BETWEEN

As I write this, today is the day my nephew was born, and his birthday just so happens to fall on the day my wife and I started dating. This day has been about pondering life, and since my father passed a little over a year ago, the day has also been about beginnings, endings, and life in between.

I think about how much of life happens outside of what we can really understand. Of all the births and incarnations happening around the world in this very moment, as I write this on this very day, I wonder what has made my nephew choose this one, this family, and these parents. So much more is going on than what we can see. What if we choose all of it? *Everything,* down to the moment we come in and the moment we go out? Life wouldn't be happening by random chance then. I think of how my wife and I came together and how perfect it is, and how even on my best, most creative day, I couldn't come up with something like that.

On one level, I have no idea what is happening or how it is happening; I can only marvel at it. On another level, there is a part of me—a deeper part of me—that is choosing it all. I don't know if that is true, and for me, that it is the most powerful way to see my life. When I went to India for the first time, my teacher proposed to us that our whole life is stamped at the moment of conception—that just as the seed of the oak tree contains the whole tree in it, so when the sperm and egg come together, the result contains the whole life of the human being; it is stamped in there.

The question then becomes, where is there choice in that? Well, it can be both chosen and determined; all is happening exactly as planned by a higher force, *and* I can also choose, moment to moment, how I want my life to unfold. So I can trust in the process. My little nephew is going to have a journey of experiences that will be similar to getting on a roller-coaster ride. There will be ups and downs, and then, in one moment, he will get off.

There seems to be a preconditioning in human beings to forget this about life, that it is all transitory. We live as if our personal life lasts forever, and we are afraid of its end. How silly is that? My father's ride ended, and my nephew's ride began, and I am somewhere in the middle, being walked home by a force that is beyond my understanding and that I can plainly see I am a part of. Not only am I part of that force, but I am an extension of it, one with it. It is here every moment for me to see. I have decided to use this life as an opportunity to awaken to it. That means not waiting until the end to realize that I am on a ride, a journey, and then looking back with regret at what I missed. Rather, I must contemplate each step, experience it, and use it for my own enlightenment. There is a part of our minds that is continuously being called to this. Maybe being born here was a detour into separation from that which we can only be connected to, and maybe, just maybe, in the forgetting, there is an opportunity for remembering. That is the opportunity each of us has. The question is, will we take it? Or will we let it pass by in hopes of something better coming along?

As an example, my marriage came out of this; of that, I am certain. Without seeking that within myself, I wouldn't have found my wife, who was in front of me, right next to me; I would've sought for something else, something of this world, in the hopes that it would fill the void of lack in me. I have tried endlessly to find that, and it has never worked, but when I sought to use everything in this world to wake up to my own wholeness, I naturally saw whatever I needed to see and found whatever I needed to find to serve that purpose. My relationship with my wife is a reminder of that, and as I look out in my life, I see all of it as a means to remember.

The question is, what is the purpose my journey will serve? What is it for? This is a question I trust my nephew will ultimately get to ask himself, and my hope for him is that his journey becomes an expression of his completeness, that he extends that gift out into the world. This ultimately is my hope for all of us.

SHORT CLIPS

What Remains?

The words I speak are my own paradigm and illustrate how the world looks for me—they are not the Truth. I'm not unique in that; you do the same thing when you speak. We speak in symbols—shapes on a page that represent an idea or object and make a sound when verbalized. Symbols will *always* be removed from the *Real Thing*. We can simply say that what I'm interested in pointing at with my words is *peace* or *love* or *joy*, but rather than call it anything, I am interested in what remains after the "sword" is put down and the warrior walks off the battlefield of the mind.

Letting Go of Conflict

I find it astonishing that in every modality I observe about the transformation of our lives, a sense of conflict shows up, no matter how enlightened the teacher and knowledge can be. It is as though they are operating from the idea of "not enough," or a competition about who is right and knows more, even though the teaching may have been the opposite. The interesting thing about it is, in the moments of heightened experience where we feel "awakened," these are the moments that can be described as unifying and as experiences of oneness.

The tricky thing about these moments is that I can have an experience of "oneness" and then go about teaching others about it without actually coming from the space of oneness with them. This explains why so-called spiritual teachers and gurus can fight among themselves and with their students, and why scandals and other crazy scenarios show up in these communities. For instance, a teacher can be about world transformation and show others that this experience is possible and believe it, but the moment someone comes to their town and attempts to teach the same thing, they can cleverly find a way to make them wrong or make up a reason why what they are talking about is superior or better in some way.

What if the entire spiritual journey of awakening is simply the letting go of conflict, competition, and superiority and coming from an open heart all the time?

The Fantasy of Happiness

I have observed that everybody wants to be happy. What attracts me to that observation is my continual search to experience my own happiness. I have looked in some interesting places. Some that I really believed would hold my happiness didn't at all when I experienced them. It's as if no experience ever lived up to the fantasy of happiness because the fantasy existed in my thinking and the experience exists in my aliveness now. This can result in a constant absence of fulfillment. For instance, when I am present during lovemaking with my wife, the lovemaking is always better. All of the times that I fantasized about being somewhere else or in a different situation that seemed somehow better at the time never lived up to the experience of being present in the moment with my love.

What if that translated in every area of life? That would mean I actually couldn't find happiness where I think or fantasize it is, but only in whatever I am doing in the present and how present I am with it. This has shown up as a constant longing to experience my childhood and the peace that I felt in those times again. For some time, I would think about this and do things in an attempt to experience it. One Christmas, I was able to watch some old footage of myself when I was a child. What was interesting about the footage was that I didn't look really joyful and happy. I had the innocence of a child, but I didn't have anything to contrast it with.

I actually find myself to be more joyful now, and the innocence of a child isn't something I need to reclaim for myself or recapture for myself to be happy. I am still that child, but with a body that is older and a personality that has more years added to it. The joy can be experienced right now. There isn't a moment when childhood ends and adulthood begins. In any moment, I can be that child and see that child in others.

Alive in the Present

I can only do what's in this moment. Life is spontaneous and flowing, whether I experience it that way or not. Being joyful and bringing joy to each moment is the greatest gift I can give to myself and to the world, beyond all of the spiritual jargon and lofty concepts. At the end of the day, I haven't seen anything outside of "what is" in the present moment, regardless of all the beautiful, touching philosophies I have come across in my lifetime. At the end of the day, or year for that matter, it doesn't really matter what I have accomplished or what I know, but whether I can be fully alive in whatever is presented in the moment.

For instance, my wife and I choose to enjoy ourselves on New Year's Eve, not having any idea what we are going to do or where we are going to be, just being alive in the present to whatever is showing up and what we are bringing. I used to strive so hard to bring in the New Year with a bang. I would throw big parties in Manhattan with all of my friends. We would have a lot of fun, but it was fleeting, the pressure leading up and the come down after. It was like I was always trying to capture a certain feeling or sensation. I saw it this year as simply the next moment. We call it a new year because of a certain date and time. When all of that is gone, it is simply this moment, simply the next moment. There is a tremendous simplicity in the recognition that there is the present moment and what I am experiencing and everything else is my own inner narrative and dialogue, to which only I am privy. I will leave you with this quote from the philosopher Democritus, "Nothing exists except atoms and empty space; everything else is opinion."

Addicted to Conflict

If someone from another time or place were to watch the lives of human beings as if they were watching a movie, they would probably conclude that human beings are addicted to conflict. Conflict is everywhere we turn, and it does seem so entrenched in our lives that it has become an expected occurrence that ultimately goes unnoticed. Some people actually wouldn't feel "loved" if some conflict didn't exist in their relationship. Based on our collective behavior, it would seem that this is "normal." What is it that propels human beings to find a certain degree of conflict normal?

Ultimately, I see that there is a part of the human spirit that treats "winning" in a conflict as if it were a matter of survival. It's as if they believe that if they can figure out a way to "win" the war of their life, mind, and heart, they will ultimately triumph and survive! I propose that to be in the war already constitutes losing. To war against something or someone requires splitting apart all of creation and deciding what can be accepted and what must ultimately be destroyed. If there is only one creation, exactly which part would be warring against the other? If one side wins, don't they both really ultimately lose?

I sometimes use the analogy of a deep-sea fish being so used to the extreme pressure at the bottom of the ocean that they would explode if they were to swim up to the surface. It seems human beings are like that. If we experienced what it would be like to live without conflict of any kind, I think we would probably explode from all that joy and freedom. It may be too much to take in all at once. Nevertheless, some of us *are* in a process or journey to become the containers for all of that love, and have decided we're taking our chances at the surface.

In the Zone

I watch people invent their lives every day; they draw experiences to them that are so specific it can hardly be called a coincidence. Sometimes it's even down to the precise details. It makes me wonder, *What does it take for that to happen?* So much has been written about this type of invention over the years that most people have some knowledge of it. The Law of Attraction books, *The Secret,* and *Think and Grow Rich,* among many others, have all attempted to explain it. Being an athlete, I have seen this "law" at work in sports. Some athletes can make it look like they are moving in slow motion or their movements are so precise that it seems as if the whole play has been choreographed. Some call this being "in the zone."

Being in the zone seems to be a key ingredient in having life turn out a certain way. Imagine what it would be like to live in such a way that it seems like everything is always working out—not necessarily *exactly* how I say it should work, but in such a way that everything that happens is for my own good and happiness. What shows up wouldn't be as important as who I am that causes such things to show up. What shows up in my life can point to whether or not I am in the zone, and that being in the zone is the most important part, rather than what is actually showing up as a result. The result shows me where I am operating from, so to that extent it is important.

Now the question becomes: What does it take for me to be in the zone? To me, when people are joyful, they are in the zone. When they are happy and playful, they are in the zone. When they are afraid and angry, they aren't in the zone. When they have a sense of lightness about life, they are in the zone. When they have a sense of heaviness and seriousness about life, they aren't in the zone. I want to be clear, emotions like anger and fear are not bad, but when they don't move through us and stay as a continued experience, they impact our effectiveness. A basketball player who is locked in fear as they shoot the free throw that can win or lose the game will not be as effective as a player who is in the zone, knowing with certainty that they have what it takes to hit the shot.

This simplifies the equation: Instead of focusing on what's happening in my life, I focus on who I am that is generating what's happening. With this very simple formula in mind, no matter what's occurring, my goal is to experience abundance, freedom, and peace. If I am experiencing something else, I can use that to practice shifting into what I want to experience. This puts me in the zone and attracts more of what I want to create in my life.

Breaking Commitments

In my experience, the topic of commitment is seldom brought up on spiritual paths or during high-level conversations. If someone says to a teacher, "I want to be enlightened," or "I want to experience the joy of my True Nature," most people wouldn't expect the teacher to start a conversation about their commitments in life—that is, the type of life, family, career and world they are committed to.

I have observed that human beings are often driven by feelings, so it makes sense that no one expects commitment to be spoken about. That's because commitment can very often be the opposite of what someone feels like doing. I have watched people use all kinds of reasons to break their commitments. Some can be as lofty as "My inner guide told me to do this" or "It's what the universe wanted." I'm not saying that these responses are never the case; maybe someone's inner guide did tell them to break a commitment. But how would they know the difference between an inner guide's instruction and a purely feeling-based decision?

When I *am* my word and surrender to commitments in life, I feel a sense of freedom and happiness. That doesn't mean it is always the easy path. How seductive would it be to say the universe or life wanted me to break this commitment?

I know that life and circumstances change, which can contribute to being or not being committed to something, but I also know that someone who has established a deep relationship with their commitment has a life that is joyful, connected, and abundant. If I behaved as if I'd made those commitments to the universe or Life itself, I might be less likely to break them. This could be why, in certain traditions, when one asks the teacher about enlightenment, the teacher starts that person with cleaning the toilets to really test their commitment, to really see how they are in the face of committing themselves to reaching enlightenment.

Our Limitation

I find beauty in the limitation of our humanness. It's as though our limitation points to something bigger, a grandeur that is elemental to us all. There is something immensely moving for me when life reminds me of that. When life shakes us, it can shake us to the core, and so much of what we thought we knew and understood loses meaning or becomes irrelevant. It is a place that is frightening for most, but to me, it is also the most promising. It promises a deeper story about life and our journey. It is a promise of peace and love that seems to be ever deepening and expanding or that has the potential to do so.

In 2015, I experienced this around death. I lost someone close to me and then right after lost my father. In many ways, I took them for granted, believing they would always be here. I found my heart aching but, at the same time, knowing there was a purpose beyond what I can see with my limited scope—that ultimately, there is no death, that life is limitless and eternal, and here I am, as a human, with all of the limitations that come with being human. I am grateful to my Creator for preparing me for things greater than I can imagine.

It's Right There

I am committed to bringing joy and excellence to my life. I declare the training I offer to be a space for people to see parts of themselves that they couldn't ordinarily see so they can then go out into their lives and use that insight as part of mastering their own journey. I have been working lately on creating a context in which people genuinely see themselves and their narratives. I am also letting go of the idea that everyone needs to "get it."

People are remarkable; they have the capacity to create in every moment, and what they are searching for is available in each moment. This is often not recognized. For instance, how many times have you or I wanted love and connection with our partner? That person is right there, the day is right there, and we have the perfect opportunity with an amazing number of moments to experience it, but somehow, we have settled for wishing for a moment "someday" or a moment in another situation that would be "better" and we convince ourselves that's what we need to experience that deeper connection, when all the while what we need is *right there*. And what if it's like that with everything—joy, love, peace, abundance, connection, and intimacy? Everything that we are seeking to access can be accessed in this moment because it is already inside us.

The Experience Itself

When human connection is centered around food and laughter, something in it touches people or makes them feel connected at their core. Sometimes this connection can be bittersweet because it brings up memories of the past, which are then compared to what is happening in the present. How many people get sad around holidays or birthdays? When we look back on past experiences, with certain ones, we tend to remember them as if they were better than they really were. We anticipate that having a similar experience will bring up those same feelings of connection we recall so fondly, if we could just re-create it.

I see this as a scam. In many cases, people believe that their memories of the past or their anticipation of something in the future are somehow better than what's happening in the present moment. However, when these things are honestly examined, this may not be true based on what actually happened or will happen. How often do we think fondly of something or someplace, and the moment we experience it, it never lives up to what we thought would happen based on our past experiences or the experience we created in our mind beforehand?

What does that say about experiencing the present? Maybe the gift is to experience the experience itself, rather than formulate a memory or anticipation of it.

Veil of "Junk"

I notice that being happy and joyful in life doesn't come easy for human beings. A veil of "junk" can cover over a person's experience of happiness. I see so many types of people on a daily basis, and I often wonder whether they experience joy and happiness.

I have witnessed many teachers talk about these great philosophies as if the mysteries of the galaxies have revealed themselves to them, and they may have success and power and all the accoutrements of the world. Still I find myself wondering, *Are they really happy?* Or maybe a better way to ask this question is: *Are they really experiencing moment-to-moment joy for themselves?*

If I knew that I was going to die tomorrow, that knowledge would change the way I participated in every single thing I did today. It would be the last day for me to be really happy and joyful—that is, if I approached my death as the amazing occurrence I believe it would be as though my whole life was preparation for that moment. My last day would be like my final holiday shopping and preparation for the big moment of celebration. (I've always loved knowing that all of my preparations for a holiday would come to fruition when we all got together to celebrate.)

It is interesting that we, as human beings, all know we are going to die, but almost everyone lives like that is never going to happen; instead, we allow our joy and happiness to get covered up by all the day-to-day "junk" we perceive is happening to us.

How many moments of our lives have we taken for

granted? How many opportunities to be totally happy and joyful have we passed up because we are under that veil of "junk"? How much intellectual posturing and jargon have we put in the way of our simple experience of joy? When we cut through everything, isn't joy what everyone is ultimately searching for?

Trust and Vulnerability

First and foremost, in my classes, I am committed to creating trust. I would like to create trust regardless of my own agenda of what I think my students should learn. I strive to create a connecting relationship with the students. Being vulnerable in front of people when I am on stage is important to me, and I am always looking to find openings to be that. Vulnerability, as I see it, is an openness with people that is beyond pretense. When I allow myself to be vulnerable, I can be myself in such a way that both the innocence of my inner child and the power of my inner guide show up.

What has made this vulnerability difficult in the past is my own personal agenda of what I think my students should learn, be, do, or have. What has also made it difficult is my desire for them to see me a certain way so I can influence and enroll them in the direction I think they should go, rather than in what is best for them. Ultimately, I don't know what is best for anyone, and when I embrace that, I find a happy lightheartedness for myself. I can still be clear on my own direction, and at the same time when I am vulnerable, it is a powerful means to allow what wants to show up in the space to come forth, rather than what I think should show up.

My Word

Arguably, the most powerful force people have in creating their lives is their word about what they say is possible and who they say they are. That is why it is so imperative for me to develop a powerful relationship with my word because there is a relationship between our word and our reality; declare something to be, and it is.

When I say "word," I don't mean just words we speak; I mean something even more fundamental than that. My "word" refers to what I think and the symbols I use—the agreements I make with others and myself. All of that is my word, and all of that is what generates my reality.

This all contributes to my ability to create in life. If I want to have an amazing life rich with possibility, I must learn to make big promises—big "words"—and keep them. It is my greatest faculty for bringing forth. The beauty is that I can practice strengthening that relationship every day. An interesting side note here is that, when someone makes a bold promise to do something within a certain period of time and they fulfill that promise right before the time is up—literally sometimes by a minute— this isn't a coincidence. Despite their procrastination, the power of their word and how much they believe in it results in how and when the promise is fulfilled. The more powerful one's belief is in their word, the quicker they fulfill their commitments to themselves and others.

Clarity and Agreement

Clear agreements are an effective structure for anyone in a relationship or on a team to create together. Trouble often shows up in relationships when people either don't have an agreement with one another or there is a lack of clarity in the agreement. I often work with couples or students who say their life or relationship isn't working, and I ask them what agreements are present in those environments that aren't being made or kept. Very often there aren't any agreements in place to begin with, or they are totally unclear. It is such a simple distinction, and yet it can be so powerful. When we are clear on our agreements, then it simply becomes about executing them or having them happen. When we are not clear, life becomes complicated from the lack of clarity, and we lose power and effectiveness with ourselves and with one another. Agreements can be as small as picking up dinner from the grocery store to as big as a vow of marriage. What is important is that the agreement itself is clear, and both parties know what fulfillment of it entails.

Strength and Power

People generally want to feel strong and powerful; entire industries revolving around money and sex have been created to validate a person's desire to feel that way. Conflict stems from a belief that one's power has been somehow lost. Why would anyone seek out power if they didn't feel weak, or at least feel that the power would give them something they don't feel they currently have?

Every struggle and suffering that I see in others as well as in myself stems from a fear of some kind of loss of power or position. What is that really about? Is loss of power even possible? Where would it go? And why is it that the people who, by the world's standards, have the most power still have fears of losing it like everyone else?

If a person can see that they are already inherently powerful and strong, then whatever happens in their life will have quite a different effect on them than it would on someone who doesn't see this. People who perceive themselves as powerful and strong—not because of some title, status, or a thing they acquired—tend to relate to their circumstances from that place. They no longer attract circumstances that continually challenge their feelings of strength and power, but rather, they attract circumstances that validate those qualities and are an expression of them.

Connected or Disconnected?

There is no end to what people will lose their peace over. These things come with such varied form and endless change that as soon as one thing is dealt with and handled, another thing takes its place. It may look like it is about everyday dilemmas, things to do or handle, but the underlying feeling of disconnect doesn't have to do with the endless list of challenges before us. It has to do with a fundamental question of who we are and whether we are connected to or disconnected from life. The reason this is so is that, in the moments when we are free, when we are certain of our oneness and whole nature, then even though the same challenges are present, there is a totally different awareness of them; there is a lightness around life, an attitude of possibility and a genuine feeling of contentment that all things and all moments contain this touch of freedom.

Seriousness and Surrender

I watch my mind grab at things, and when it does, seriousness creeps in. There is a temptation to regard circumstances in life as something I would let go of my peace of mind for and be resistant to. I also see that there can be a surrender on the other side of that seriousness. Everyone has the option to choose between those two experiences. *A Course in Miracles* says it perfectly: "Reason will tell you that the only way to escape from misery is to recognize it and go the other way!" In any moment, I can choose either misery or peace, each of which is available to me, whether or not I recognize it.

Overwhelm

The whole idea of overwhelm is a myth. I had an experience recently of overwhelm, so I wrote everything down on paper that I could think of that I needed to accomplish.

It was almost laughable that what I "needed" to do had overwhelmed me. Overwhelm seems to be a fear of the unknown and the future, which creates a level of disengagement to what is here now. The only fact I can see in all of it is that everyone can only do what they are doing in this moment. Whether they are present to it or present to a sense of overwhelm are two entirely different conversations. We can only engage in this moment, and the irony is that overwhelm takes us out of this moment, puts us into the past or future, and thereby lessens our effectiveness at getting something done in *this* moment.

Instant Shift

It can take just one instant for someone's life to shift direction, and there can be a long journey to that instant. It may seem like a lot of "work" has been done in dealing with the situation, whatever it is. A feeling of wrestling with it, of struggling with it, and then all it takes is an instant, and one's life can shift. There is often a downward momentum when things don't feel like they are fitting together, and then BAM! It's like something takes over and is revealed as though it was perfectly planned the whole time. Seeing that happen in my life and the lives of others creates a possibility of remembering that we *are* being guided, even during those times when it doesn't feel like it.

Our Own Hero

We have come from a long history of idolizing certain people for what appears to be a higher knowledge or skill set in life; we believe they have "more" than the average person. I believe it is time to usher in a new era where each person is regarded as the sage or hero of their own life's journey and every human being has the potential for greatness and awakening within themselves. I believe we need not a hierarchy of teacher and followers, but an understanding that each person has the possibility of insight and wisdom within them, and in many ways, we are all teachers and students for each other.

Freedom from Conflict

Before we attempt to solve the issue of conflict in the world, it is imperative to come to terms with the battle that is taking place within us. Freedom is freedom from conflict; when there is war in our hearts and minds, we aren't free. What I see outside myself is a reflection of my own internal narrative about life. Anything that shows up that puts me in conflict with the outer world can be a great pointer to the fight that is already there inside me. The fundamental split in my mind between conflict and peace will be healed only when I see that I valued this split and what I believed it would give me in this world. So let's first notice the fundamental problems in our own minds and hearts before we attempt to solve a million different problems outside ourselves.

The Beginner's Mind

People are usually unaware of the prices they are paying and the payoffs they are getting for the way they see life and what they do in life. What I mean by a *payoff* is short-term pleasure that generates long-term pain. A payoff may be seeking approval, being right, or the constant need to be in control. A *price* then is something that a perspective or action costs me, and it's usually something that I really want, such as love, health, or abundance. When given a direct opportunity to see this, people place themselves in a space of choice, but until then, how can they speak of choice when they're aren't clear on what is driving their behavior and thinking?

Another difficulty arises in thinking we already know what everything is. We live in what we know rather than in the question. That's why the beginner's mind is so important; with it, we can look honestly at what causes our interpretation in any given moment, instead of presuming we know. There is what is, and there is the meaning I bring to it and the payoffs I get and the prices I pay for bringing that specific meaning to it. The extent to which people can be aware of this is the extent to which they can be powerful, effective creators in their lives. I choose to stand in the question of not knowing the answers, to use this question to shape my journey, and to always stay a beginner.

Stories and Reactions

When someone is in reaction to life, they cannot see the neutrality of events. Perhaps the most difficult thing to realize is that no event ever causes our reaction. To realize that, we would have to fess up to what we tell ourselves about what events mean. Until we are willing to look at the perceived benefit we think we're getting from telling ourselves a specific story, we won't be willing to surrender that narrative. Even if we let it go, we will create a similar reaction to another situation. The key is to address the stories and the payoffs we get that are generating our reaction rather than address the events we think caused the reaction.

Borrowed Time

There is something beautifully sobering about the fact that, in less than a hundred years from now, almost every single human experience that is happening currently on this planet, and every belief anyone has about anything, will not be there. Now, I'm not presuming to know what the experience after this physical form will be, or even if there is an experience in the way we think of it; every statement about what happens to us when we transcend this form is made on an assumption. There may be great pointers that end up being true, but no one ultimately knows what lies beyond in the Great Mystery. I find something beautiful about that because we are all on borrowed time. I mean, who even remembers what happened in this hour on this day during this month five years ago? So many moments span across a life, and yet they all end up in the same place. For some, that can be frightening and depressing, and for others it can be beautifully liberating. I guess the question is, which will it be for me, and what will the purpose of my life be with my borrowed time?

Putting One's House in Order

J. Krishnamurti, a well-known teacher, said, "The mind that has put its house in order is silent." When completion happens, there is space. Resistance and fear generate avoidance. We try to avoid these things, instead of approaching and mastering how we relate to them. There is a loud, raucous noise that comes from all of the incompletions in life. They continually bark at me. To me, putting one's house in order means confronting and completing one's life in such a way that is masterful. Rather than resisting and avoiding those places in our life that need to be completed, we must approach them for the purpose of mastering them. Then, silence and peace become a natural byproduct of mastery, a natural byproduct of a life that works.

Stop and Ask

In any moment, we can call in a force higher than ourselves for guidance. We are not separate from that force, but in the moment when it seems like we are locked in fear or suffering and can't access that force within us, there is a space that can be opened up by the part of our mind that remembers—when we simply stop and ask. In my experience, no matter what the situation, that space is always available to us. The question is, do we have the presence of mind to stop and ask? For most people, that "voice" (a thought, idea, or feeling) is difficult to hear because they are too busy listening to their own voice, which is the loud yelling of the ego. The humility comes from recognizing that we need guidance, and the strength comes in asking for it. Presence of mind is available to us in any moment we choose for it to be, and once we are aware of the need for guidance, then all it takes is stopping and asking for it to be heard.

Happily Ever After

I'm not sure it serves people to believe the idea that, somehow, there will be a moment in life of such clarity and knowing that they will never experience anything else and they'll live happy ever after. I've believed it at times, but what I've found is that experiencing love and happiness is a gradual, slow-cooking type of process. Allowing the experience to happen is something that can be developed, like a muscle of the mind that guides how we see the world. When this is understood, it is easier to have compassion for people who, in this moment, might not be experiencing love and happiness. It's also easier to see that "happily ever after" is not something that will occur in some distant future but exists in every moment.

The Work Is in the Moment

Spiritual experiences themselves will never give us the peace and contentment we are looking for. Whether it is a ten-day silent retreat, plant ceremonies, meditation, breathwork, or any other vehicle, they all may be a great reminder or a view into other realms, but at the end of the day, we come back as ourselves—maybe with some powerful insights, but even those seem to fade over time as daily life sets in. That's where the work really is: in the day-to-day, moment-to-moment opportunities where we can begin to develop ourselves as the type of beings who live in the states that we have previously only seen in mystical experiences. Love ultimately is the strongest practice, and our daily life is the playing field.

TO MY GUIDE

It turns out you could see this in me all along. I thank you for that. Where I was afraid and thought I would need to sacrifice myself for the journey, I find a happy lightheartedness instead. When you spoke to me about the illusory nature of things and the world, even though I felt the truth in what you spoke, I knew it to be illusory only intellectually. I was still rebelling against that in my heart, as being attached to the world and the way I wanted it to be. I am grateful for what I am and what all beings inherently are. I now get to bring a grateful heart back to the world.

I acknowledge myself for my earnestness and for how it has served me. I know no experience will ultimately last, and that the journey continues. In some way, so much has changed, and in other ways, nothing has; I'm still a traveler on a journey that may continue for a long time, even beyond this life. The one thing that I know has shifted for sure is that I am honoring the journey, whereas before I wanted it to be over. In fact, at times, I was angry that it had even begun. I can now see these oppositions and challenges are of my own making, and I release them in exchange for a deeper level of forgiveness and compassion within myself. My vision is to extend that forgiveness and compassion to all beings now, to have my life be a reminder for them also.

When I started the journey, in the beginning it felt like I was trying to zero in on Truth or God, like I was honing in on something. Now, it feels like those two arrows that were at once attempting to hone in on Truth are pointing outward toward everything on the journey as a part of God or Truth. I see that being possible in every situation. In every moment, it is possible for me to remember. I am sure there will be times when I forget this, but I trust in my ability and willingness to always come around.

I want to be a beacon of light for the world around me and, in recognizing the majesty of my own mind, to inspire people to wake up to the majesty of their own. Through our work, I see that I am *it*—that throughout this whole process, I was looking for my Self in everything. I survived the dark times when I confronted everything I put in the way of my own Self, and although there were times it seemed like it would never end, it most certainly did. It was like a cloud that was blocking the sun but eventually passed. I realize now that no cloud can ever put out the sun in me, and I have hope for remembering that when I attempt to put a cloud over it again.

I trust in all I have learned that has made me a courageous journeyer, and I thank you for being the One to guide the way back home. I am forever grateful to you, and I realize the greatest way I can repay it to you is to give what you have given me to the world. Thank you.

Sincerely,
Christopher, Urban Mystic

AS FOR WHAT'S NEXT

Something that always gave me solace whenever I faced bumps on the path is that everything—all of the powerful teachings spoken about—was what I already am. I didn't have to go far to find it. It is always here. The same goes for you. You are magnificent, the creation of God. I honor you as my Self. I look forward to sharing what is next on our journey together. I acknowledge you for coming this far with me.

Keep an eye out for what is next from the Urban Mystic. Visit www.ChristopherDeSanti.com.

ACKNOWLEDGMENTS

First and foremost, I would like to thank God, the Source, the Creator of all things in form. I seek every day to recognize my connection with You. Without which I would not exist. You have been called by many names but still remain the nameless.

Next, I would like to acknowledge all of my teachers many of whom I have never met in physical form. Their words inspire me every day and much of what is written in this book is because I was fortunate to stand on their shoulders. Ramana Maharishi, Nisargadatta Maharaj, Bhagwan Nityananda of Ganeshpuri, and many many others. Too many to name here. I feel I owe a debt of gratitude to all of them. Their faces and words are with me very often. Thank you, Ram Dass, for opening the door.

I would also like to acknowledge my coaches and mentors of recent years that were instrumental in me understanding at a deeper level. My trainer mentors Dr. Ray Blanchard and Bettie Spruill, I am grateful for your wisdom and guidance. I am who I am as a trainer today because of you. John Hanley, Sr., thank you for being a visionary and a friend.

Also to all of the trainers who have impacted my life; and to Barry Warren and Gerard Hauranieh, my trainer colleagues and friends.

My coach Gary Grant, I appreciate all I have learned from your unique perspective during our coaching calls over the last five years. I am sure you can see many of our talks echoed in these pages.

To Jo and Francine, my transformational sisters. I couldn't imagine my life without us working together. Our stand together inspires me and I know it impacts the world.

To my family and friends, thank you for the continued love and guidance. I appreciate all of you.

To my mother and my brothers, we have defintely come far. I love our journey together more than words can express. Thank you.

Thank you to all who supported in this book, specifically the Book Couple, Carol and Gary Rosenberg.

And lastly, to the one who is the soil for all of this, my wife, Lori. You are the inspiration for so many things in my life. The level that you get me is profound, and I am grateful we chose each other. I love you.

∞

ABOUT THE AUTHOR

Christopher DeSanti is an international transformational trainer and educator of higher knowledge. A seeker of this knowledge since childhood, he participated in Native American shamanic teachings throughout his late teens and was later drawn to the teachings of the Masters of India. Christopher, who is known as an Urban Mystic, has spent over two decades studying, meditating, and reflecting on the words and practices of this rich lineage. His encounter with *A Course in Miracles*, combined with teachings of nonduality, enabled him to help other seekers discover the cause of the suffering in their own lives. In 2008, he began facilitating his own Satsang-style classes and continues to hold private classes each week.

After attending Gratitude Training in 2011, a transformative three-part course, he went on to become an International Trainer after three years of intense immersion in the training. He was fortunate to learn from two pioneer Trainers, both of whom were instrumental in creating the work and who are standing members on the Transformation Leadership Council. Christopher is currently a director of and facilitates trainings for Gratitude

Training, LLC, where he brings his wisdom and passion to his classes, with commitment to and love for people from all walks of life. Thousands have had the opportunity to experience his unique, innovative, and powerful teaching style.

He currently resides in Delray Beach, Florida, and spends his time with his graceful and loving wife, Lori. Together they have created a beautiful relationship that has become a source of inspiration for many. Christopher uses his relationship and many other day-to-day life experiences as the basis of what he teaches and shares with people, creating a safe and relatable environment for people to ask the deeper questions about existence. Visit www.ChristopherDeSanti.com to learn more about the Urban Mystic.

Made in the
USA
Lexington, KY

54722657R00079